Regression, Past-Life Therapy for Here and Now Freedom

Clairvision™

PO Box 33, Roseville NSW 2069, Australia
Web site: http://clairvision.org/
E-mail: info@clairvision.org

By the same author:

* **Awakening the Third Eye**

* **Entities, Parasites of the Body of Energy**

* **Planetary Forces, Alchemy and Healing**

* **Clairvision Astrology Manual**
  This electronic manual can be obtained from the Clairvision School's Internet address.

* **Subtle Bodies – The Fourfold Model**
  A book accompanied by 12 cassettes.

To be published in 1997:
Atlantean Secrets
An epic novel on the origins of the Clairvision tradition and the spiritual grandeur and downfall of Atlantis. This work comes in four volumes:

* **Atlantean Secrets, Vol. 1 – Sleeper, Awaken!**

* **Atlantean Secrets, Vol. 2 – Forever Love, White Eagle**

* **Atlantean Secrets, Vol. 3 – The Gods are Wise**

* **Atlantean Secrets, Vol. 4 – The Return of the Flying Dragon.**

Contact Clairvision for a list of all available texts, cassettes and other learning material.

Regression, Past-Life Therapy for Here and Now Freedom

Dr Samuel Sagan

Cover by Steve Goldsmith

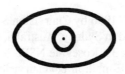

Clairvision™

PO Box 33, Roseville NSW 2069, Australia
Web site: http://clairvision.org/
E-mail: info@clairvision.org

Acknowledgments

Many thanks to the editors and correctors who have worked on the manuscript of this book: Catherine Ross, Rosa Droescher, Orna Lankry, Jonathan Marshall, Anne and Michael Barbato, Peter Twigg, David McKenzie.

Table of Contents

INTRODUCTION

Regression is one of the great techniques of the future in the fields of self-discovery and psychotherapy. One of its essential characteristics is that it integrates two dimensions within the same process: a psycho-therapeutic dimension, and a metaphysical one.

To psychotherapists, regression is a transpersonal technique allowing explorations and releases of unprecedented depth, and through which a much needed metaphysical dimension can be incorporated into psychotherapy.

To spiritual seekers, regression is a major tool in the opening of perception, a powerful awakener of the third eye, and above all a path of mental de-conditioning. It achieves a profound and systematic purification of the emotional layer – not unlike the catharsis which Bernard de Clairveaux, patron of the Templars, used to describe with the Latin word *defæcatio*, considering it an indispensable preliminary to higher spiritual experience.

Regression aims at exploring and releasing emotional blockages and mental complexes, as do many other therapies. The specificity of regression, however, lies in its unsurpassed capacity to reach hidden subconscious and unconscious memories. Even in the first sessions, it is not uncommon to experience flashbacks that cannot be related to any experience in this life, but are accompanied by a deep feeling and an inner certitude that they refer to yourself. Hence the name 'past-life therapy' is often given to regression.

Regarding past lives, however, a few points must be made clear right from the beginning. First, it is in no way necessary to believe in past lives to undergo a regression process. ISIS, the regression technique which I have developed, uses neither imagination nor creative visualisation. It does not ask you to believe anything, just to follow a process. Actually the fewer beliefs you bring with you, the more chance of success, for beliefs generate expectations that tend to distort the purity of the experiences.

Some of the flashbacks during regression have an extreme clarity and leave the client with little doubt that they are real. Yet what matters with regression experiences is not whether they come from past lives, but what sort of improvement they can bring to your present. To use the words of one of my clients just after completing an intense regression: "I don't know about past lives, but as far as *my* life is concerned, this certainly makes a lot of sense!" What matters is how the client's present life can be changed, and not so much the origin of the experience. Let people decide for themselves what the real nature of these flashbacks may be. However, readers would be poorly inspired to try to make up their mind before undergoing regressions themselves, for the intensity and sharpness of the flashbacks are far greater than most people imagine when they think of past-life therapy. Moreover, some regressions are accompanied by a 'flavour of the Self' – a sense of your own continuity in time that words are powerless to describe as long as you have not gone through the experience yourself.

A second essential point is that the purpose of the ISIS method of regression is not to write a novel about your past lives, but to work at clearing the present. Regression is concerned with the client's *present* emotional and mental blockages, and how to release them. It may lead to reexperiencing episodes of early childhood, or possibly certain episodes that cannot be related to any event of this present life. However, if clients start to be more interested in the details of past-life stories than in how the regression can help them become freer and more awakened, then the process can quickly become meaningless, and moreover invite all kinds of delusions. This warning is essential and will therefore be repeated several times throughout the book. The goals of ISIS are deconditioning, emotional freedom here and now, and Self-awareness. ISIS aims at unveiling your real nature, and cares little about who you have been.

Thirdly, my intention in this book is not to argue or 'demonstrate' the reality of past lives. Actually I do not believe that one can prove the reality of past lives, just as there is absolutely no way one can prove the reality of dreams. It happens that nearly everybody remembers their dreams, at least from time to time, so that there is little doubt about whether they exist or not. But suppose you were living in a world where no one but you remembered dreams.

Introduction

How could you prove their reality? Each time you told your story, most people would immediately answer "Nonsense!" You could try to produce an EEG showing that your brain wave patterns were altered each time you dreamt. But then the sceptics would argue this only proved that your brain waves change, and that there was no need to invent something as fanciful as dreams in order to explain the phenomenon.

Similarly, only direct experience can bring a real understanding of the subject of past lives. It is better to show techniques which allow this direct experience, and let time do its sublime work. As Einstein used to say, it is rare that people let themselves be convinced by new ideas. What happens is that the people with the old ideas eventually die, and those who follow them find the new ideas very natural and adopt them. Once a sufficient proportion of the population has gone through the type of flashbacks that occur during regression, it seems quite probable that past-life experiences will become as common and accepted as dreams.

Once, I was invited to speak about regression to a society who had contacted me after reading one of my articles in a health magazine. I accepted without further enquiry. I arrived at their place a quarter of an hour early and, after their secretary gave me a polite but distant welcome, I decided to spend the time that was left reading the pamphlets of the organisation. It immediately became clear that I had landed among a group of sceptics who had invited me only to attack my views. A short but intense moment of cogitation followed, during which I had to find a new strategy and change the format of my lecture.

I spoke to them in the following way (and I would ask sceptical readers to view this book in the same manner): "Here are the case studies of a number of my clients. Here are the words they have said when going through these flashbacks. I do not pretend that this demonstrates or proves anything. Still, some kind of new experience must be emerging, because other regressors and I have observed similar patterns in thousands of sessions. It is up to you to draw your own conclusions. To me, what really matters is that after these regressions the clients get better. Not all, of course, but a significant number. They get rid of tranquillisers and sleeping tablets. They find it easier to relate to others, and their general level of neurosis decreases. A number of them even undergo a deep transformation and change of values. Some adopt a much more philosophical attitude towards life and begin to question their purpose on Earth."

By not trying to convince them of anything, I took the sceptics by surprise. As a result, they proved surprisingly receptive. We laughed a lot at the awkward character of some of my case studies, and their president concluded the evening by saying that, after all, their society was in favour of any technique that allowed one to empty the garbage cans of the mind – which is exactly what regression does.

More than a new technique, regression is a new experience, or rather the dissemination of an old experience in proportions unknown until now. Throughout history, from the Indian *rsis* to Goethe via Plato and an uninterrupted line of 'seers', there have always been individuals who recalled experiences of former incarnations on Earth. But these experiences were rare. In the last fifteen years, I have witnessed major changes in the way people gain access to past-life flashbacks (or whatever you may decide to call the experiences).

When I was practising regression in the early nineteen eighties, I had to confine my clients to a house for two weeks, implementing the techniques non-stop. The process was drastic and could only be undergone by people who had reached a certain degree of emotional stability through years of working on themselves. Usually, it was only after seven or ten days spent building up the inner pressure that some of the participants would start having regression experiences.

Now, in the mid-nineties, the situation has become quite different. Residential courses are no longer needed. Weekly private sessions of one or two hours are sufficient. Some clients, when lying down in my practice room for the first time, even start regressing before I have finished implementing my techniques! The process has become relatively smooth and gentle, and therefore open to virtually everyone. Moreover, the regressions all these people experience are often deeper and more genuine than those of their predecessors fifteen years ago. Obviously something has changed. More and more frequently one hears of people who go and see their acupuncturist for a sore neck or some other minor problem, and unexpectedly experience a momentous past-life flash as soon as the needles are placed on their body – even though neither they nor their acupuncturist knew anything about regression. Of course, these remain relatively isolated cases, and it would not be correct to expect that you are going to know your past lives with a snap of the fingers; any work of quality takes time and effort. Still, access to the regression state has become infinitely easier than it used to be, which could end up having considerable consequences not only on different fields of therapy, but on some of the very foundations of our society.

ISIS, connector and client

The ISIS technique of regression is based on three main principles:

1) the **inner space** of the third eye, contacted through the area between the eyebrows;

2) the **interaction** between two people, one who lies down and undergoes the regression experience, and the other who sits close by and monitors the energy during the session. The first one is called the '**client**', and the second the '**connector**';

3) **sourcing**, that is, systematically looking for the source of all emotional imprints and behavioural conditioning.

The initials of the three terms, Inner Space Interactive Sourcing, happily combine into ISIS.

It must be stressed that the ISIS technique does not use any form of hypnotic suggestion or hyperventilation. It operates through an activation of the body of energy, and in particular the third eye. It therefore leads to a completely new perception of your emotions as forms and waves in your consciousness. This structural perspective will provide several opportunities throughout the book to explore certain basic mechanisms related to subtle bodies and their destiny after death.

Clairvision School
PO BOX 33
Roseville NSW 2069
Australia
Web site: http://clairvision.org/
E-mail: info@clairvision.org

CHAPTER 1

THE MECHANISMS OF SAMSKARAS

Samskara is one of the most important Sanskrit terms in Hindu philosophy. Yoga, the union with the Higher Self, is said to be achieved as soon as the last samskara has been worked out. Therefore the primary objective of all yogas, or paths of self transformation, is to eradicate the samskaras of the mind. This is why it is so important for those who to want to know themselves, or rather their Self, to have a clear vision of all the mechanisms of their samskaras.

1.1 The fundamental mechanism

You have a car accident at a particular place. Then, for a long while, each time you drive past that place you feel uneasy; a wave of fear arises. You may even feel uncomfortable just by thinking of the episode. The traumatic imprint left in your mind after the accident is called a samskara. The malaise that subsequently appears each time you drive past the place is called a reactional emotion, or more simply an emotion. The tendency of the samskara to generate a wave of fear whenever remembering the accident is called the dynamism of the samskara.

Basically, all samskaras operate in the same way. Simple. Yet, according to the Upanishads, the final chapters of the Vedas, as soon as the last knot of samskaras in the heart has been untied, the highest state of consciousness is cognised, absolute freedom is reached, and *martyo 'mṛto bhavati*, "the mortal becomes immortal".[1]

---

[1] Katha-Upanishad 6.15 and Brihad-Aranyaka-Upanishad 4.4.7.

1.2 How could we define a samskara?

Samskaras are the tracks left in the mind by previous traumatic experiences. Roughly speaking, samskaras are the 'scars' of the mind. (The association samskara-scar is easy to remember.) In the fourfold model of subtle bodies used in this book, the layer of the mind corresponds to the astral body.[1] Samskaras can therefore be regarded as imprints or scars in the astral body, as will be examined in detail throughout this book.

Let us consider a few examples to clarify the concept of samskara. If a woman is raped by her father when she is sixteen years old, it leaves a track in her psychological organisation, and this track is a samskara. Her way of relating to men will never be the same again. In various life situations, this track will deeply influence her emotional behaviour. This means that the samskara is neither neutral nor mute. Rather, it is endowed with a powerful dynamism – an emotional charge. It generates emotions, attractions and repulsions that will significantly modify the inner life of this person. Being associated with such traumatic and painful memories, the samskara cannot remain silent; it *has* to express itself in a conscious or unconscious way. This applies to *all* samskaras – not just a few particular cases. Whether you realise it or not, in the depths of yourself your samskaras are perpetually crying out to be healed.

Now suppose that this woman, instead of being raped at the age of sixteen, was assaulted when she was three. Her experience was even more terrifying and traumatic, because as a little girl she had no way of understanding what was happening. To her, the assault was like a murder. But the shock was so unbearable that she forgot everything, completely wiping out the episode from her conscious memory. The samskara has been stored with an even greater emotional charge than in the case of the sixteen-year-old girl; but in this case, the samskara is completely unconscious. Later on as an adult, her entire emotional and sexual life will be undermined by a hidden trauma of which she is completely unaware. She may run away from men, or run after men, or display all sorts of irrational behaviour against her own free will. She may develop a major dis-

---

[1] This simple model comprising physical body, etheric body, astral body and Higher Ego is outlined in section 4.3.

ease in the pelvic region, or miscarry when she tries to have a child. Without a process that allows her to explore the depths of her unconscious, she will never be able to understand why her life is such a mess. Any attempt to reorganise her existence will be doomed from the start, for she is missing the main piece of her personal puzzle.

Up to this point, all that has been envisaged fits into psychoanalytic models and common psychological modes of understanding quite well. Further, one could ponder on the fact that Sanskrit texts were already discussing these topics a few thousand years before Freud. But a major difference is encountered when practising regression – clients discover a number of samskaras that cannot be related to any experience from their present life.

Case study – Twenty-two-year-old woman. During the beginning of the ISIS session, a very sore spot was revealed in the stomach area. After twenty or thirty minutes spent implementing the technique, the client became very quiet and serene, and started to reexperience the following episode.[1]

What are you feeling? –It just looks stale and grey. It feels very defeated. A woman with her head hanging between her shoulders, backward. She is quite young, with long hair, and a white dress. I can't see her face.
Does she feel happy, or sad? –She is *very* sad.
Is she crying? –No.
Does it feel warm or cold around her? –Cold.
Is there any noise? –No. It is dead silent. She is really tired. It feels tighter now in the stomach.
What does she want? –She wants something back that she has lost. She knows she can't do anything.
Is she alone? –Yes. She is very young. She is wounded.
Physically wounded? –Yes.
Does she feel any pain? –She has lost a lot of blood. But she doesn't care. She is very cold.

---

[1] The questions at the beginning of the paragraphs are asked by the connector. The answers are those given by the client.

Can you feel her pain? –It starts in the stomach, in the ribcage and it goes to the back, between the shoulder blades. She can feel her heart beat. She has regrets. Her family is gone and they can't come back. She just wants to die.

Her family? –A man. And her child. Her child was three. He had soft curly hair... It was an attack. The man was very strong, so he was taken somewhere.

And the child? –The child was killed. He died in front of her.

How? –It was very difficult, very cruel. She does not remember much of that.

How did he die? –A spear through him. Her lips have turned blue... The woman was assaulted too.

What did they do to her? –About six soldiers.

What did they look like? –Dark coats, short hair, with helmets. Something on top of the helmets. No beard. They were dark-skinned. Shorter than the man.

What did they do to her? –I don't know. She does not remember. It does not matter.

Try to see. –Four men held her. It is hard to say. They held her and raped her just near the child's body.

Was he dead? –Yes.

And then? –When they finished, the last one kicked her in the stomach and in the ribs. That is why she can taste blood in her mouth.

And then? –She crawls back into her house... And she dies a moment later.

As is often the case, this samskara was buried and the young woman had never suspected its presence before. Yet it was not buried that deeply, since it could be brought back to the surface and re-experienced in this regression, which was only the second in the process. Being endowed with such a dramatic emotional charge, the samskara could not possibly remain neutral and inactive. One year before the regressions took place, this young woman had lost a child by miscarrying a few weeks before her delivery. While undergoing the regression, she immediately recognised that the pain she had felt at the time of the miscarriage was exactly the same as the woman's pain when she was raped and her son killed.

The superimposition of the two episodes is indeed puzzling. It is as if a drama of the past had to be replayed because the wounds it had left had not been healed. Without realising that this samskara was buried in her unconscious and influencing her, what chance was there for this young woman to understand what was happening in her present? In cases like this one, it is hard to know whether the miscarriage would still have happened, had the regressions been carried out before the pregnancy. However, as soon as the client discovered this samskara, her life started changing. Her sadness abated, and the emotional wound left by the miscarriage started to heal. She regained a certain centredness and a greater sense of purpose.

1.3 Are samskaras always associated with negative experiences?

The criterion for a major samskara to be imprinted is not pain, but intensity. Strong samskaras are engraved in the astral body when an episode is associated with emotional intensity. We all know from our own experience in this life that we tend to be too unhappy more often than too happy. The same can be expected to have taken place in former lives. This explains why major samskaras surfacing from our past have statistically more chance of being related to painful events than to joyful ones. Yet any intense joy can create a samskara, in much the same way as Chinese medicine considers joy can induce a heart attack.

Case study – Twenty-four-year-old man.

–I am in a very small space, like metal all around me. There is vibration, a metallic vibration... I see all these people. I know I am wounded on my right side but I don't even feel it. I am completely exhausted, annihilated. And at the same time it feels GOOD! As if I had been fighting for three days and three nights non-stop. It feels so... beyond everything. There is nothing left of me, there is just the sky.
–It's a cockpit. I'm in a plane. I can hear the noise; and there is the vibration. The plane is going to land. It's more than being worn out, it's like seeing everything from a distance.

10

–There is a shock when the plane reaches the ground. And I can see all these people, a crowd waiting for me. There is a feeling of glory... Oh! my God! It is huge. In my heart, an IMMENSE feeling of glory. I don't know what I have done, but they seem to like it very much. It's war...

–My plane has landed and they are all waving their arms. They run towards the plane. Oh! my God! [starting to cry] I think that now I'm cracking up. I have not slept for a long, long, long time... I did not know one could feel glory that big.

1.4 How do emotions intensify samskaras?

There are several reasons why a samskara is imprinted much more deeply in your structure if it is accompanied by an intense emotion. Suppose you are going to be beheaded. The experience will leave a more profound impression in your psyche than if you were going to visit your hairdresser. You can go to an appointment with your hairdresser mindlessly and daydreaming, without being really concerned. You cannot go to your execution without feeling concerned. You may have forgotten many visits paid to your hairdresser but if you escape the dungeon, there is no way you will ever forget it, because in the dungeon you are in the very opposite of a mindless state. All your senses are wide open. You are utterly aware and vigilant. It is not a blurry cloud that is imprinted in your memory, but a sharp and precise package of thoughts, feelings and perceptions. If you get out of it alive, even thirty years later, you will be able to re-member every single detail. Every bit of information will be stored: what the place looked and felt like, the colours on the walls, every noise and smell, all your emotions and feelings. And if you end up dying in the dungeon, you will keep this package of memories with you as one of the most vivid of this entire life, and will carry it with you into the lives that follow.

1.5 Are all samskaras created by major events or emotions?

Some major samskaras can be created by quite minor events, for the samskara is not due to the event itself, but to your emotional reaction to it. For instance, a child can be completely terrified by an animal. To the child, even a tame dog can suddenly turn into a terrible and life-threatening monster and cause an irrational panic fear, thereby generating a strong samskara. Conversely, some people remain emotionally stable in the most dramatic circumstances and, therefore, go through intense events without any major samskara being imprinted.

1.6 Micro-samskaras and samskaras proper

So far we have only considered the samskaras that are endowed with strong emotional charges. Apart from these major imprints, myriads of minor ones are also stored in your mind.

The input you are constantly receiving from your sense organs is kept in subconscious parts of the mind. You know the details are not lost because they can be recalled in your memory at any time, if triggered by the appropriate stimulus. For instance, you arrive at a place where a certain smell is wafting in the air, and suddenly a connection is made with a remote episode of your past. In a fraction of a second you are transported back into a room where you had been thirty years ago. The colours, the sounds, the atmosphere of that room are brought back to your consciousness, because the smell in it was similar to that which you are sensing now. This recollection does not take place because of any dramatic event that happened to you in the room. The situation was quite ordinary, and no particular emotion or pain was experienced. The same mechanism often takes place with an old song or a piece of music that can immediately transport you back to a part of your past, recalling all the corresponding emotions and feelings.

In this pattern, one can recognise the characteristics of samskaras. A package of sensory impressions gets imprinted in your subconscious or conscious mind. It is stored there without your knowing it, but it is still vivid, since it can be retrieved at any time. When the right stimulus is met, such as the smell, or the piece of music, the imprint is triggered and a **reaction** takes place. You reexperience sensations, emotions and feelings related to this particular part of your past.

1.7 What is the difference between karma and samskara?

The literal meaning of the Sanskrit word karma is action. Karma refers to all the actions you have performed in your past, both in this life and in former ones. The mechanisms of karma are such that each action you perform is like an impulse you send out into the universe. After a lapse of time that can vary greatly (up to more than a few lives!), the impulse comes back to you like a boomerang and generates corresponding circumstances in your life. Negative deeds tend to create unfavourable circumstances when the corresponding impulse returns, whilst positive actions come to fruition in auspicious conditions. This is the aspect of the theory of karma which is straightforward and which everybody more or less agrees with. However, not everyone agrees on how directly the circumstances of the past reflect into the present. Will those who have killed by the sword *have* to perish by the sword? As far as this question is concerned, very enlightened people have held quite different views.[1]

Samskaras are of a completely different nature. Instead of being external waves sent to you by the universe, they are internal factors. More precisely, they are **emotional imprints** left inside your unconscious mind, and which in turn tend to influence your present emotional responses.

Another major difference lies in the fact that some insignificant karmas (actions) can be associated with huge samskaras (emotional scars), for example when a little boy is gripped with panic when meeting the neighbours' well-meaning German Shepherd, or when a baby is terrified by a storm. Although in these instances there is virtually no action, that is, no significant karma, there may be enough samskara for the child to display neurotic symptoms for the rest of his life. Conversely, the most heinous crimes – representing big bad karma – can be committed coldly and mindlessly, without any deep samskaras being imprinted.[2]

---

[1] See two essential references on the topic of karma: Steiner, Rudolf, *Karmic Relationships*, Rudolf Steiner Press, London, (8 volumes); Aurobindo, Sri, *The Problem of Rebirth*, Sri Aurobindo Ashram, Pondicherry, 1952.

[2] Those who have practised *vipassana*, the Buddhist technique of meditation, have probably heard a lot about the *sammkaras*, which are the

1.8 Do animals also have samskaras?

Since animals can become neurotic, we can assume they also have samskaras. The reflexes observed by Pavlov in his work with dogs present clear analogies with the conditioning of the samskaras.

Another important Sanskrit word related to samskaras is manas. Manas refers to the layer in which we think and experience emotions. More precisely, manas has to do with the thoughts and emotions which are reactions directly related to samskaras. The concept of 'reacting mind' (manas) will be developed at length later in the book.

Manas is usually translated into English as 'mind'. The English word 'mind', however, is used by different people with quite different meanings. In the context of the Clairvision work, I use the word mind with the meaning of 'reacting mind', which is the same as that of the Sanskrit word manas, the layer in which reactional thoughts and emotions take place. There are several reasons for this choice, as will become apparent later.

When defined in this way, the mind corresponds quite precisely to what Rudolf Steiner calls the astral body.[1] In the present context, the reader can equate all the following terms:

**mind = reacting mind = manas = manas/mind
= layer of the samskaras = astral body**

At times, however, distinctions will be established between the astral body, which is a vehicle of consciousness, and the reacting

---

exact equivalent of samskaras. The difference in spelling comes from the fact that *vipassana* belongs to Hinayana Buddhism, whose texts were written in Pali – a language which is derived from Sanskrit. Many Sanskrit words have been reshaped in Pali so that when two consonants follow one another, the latter is transformed into the former. Thus 'ms' is turned into 'mm', and *samskara* in Sanskrit becomes *sammkara* in Pali. Similarly 'sy' becomes 'ss', and the Sanskrit word *vipashyana* (discerning or penetrating vision), becomes *vipassana* in Pali.

[1] Defined in this way, 'mind' corresponds quite exactly to the Greek *dianoia*, as opposed to *nous*. Mind can also be equated with the Latin *ratio*, as opposed to *intellectus*.

mind, which is the mental consciousness taking place within this vehicle.

From the point of view of the Hindu tradition, animals do have a manas/mind, just as according to Rudolf Steiner, they do have an astral body. Animals can associate facts mentally and draw conclusions, as when a mouse finds its way out of a maze. Animals also experience emotions such as anger and jealousy. Since the astral body, in which the samskaras are imprinted, is not a specifically human attribute but also pertains to animals, samskaras could even be described as a part of ourselves that we have in common with animals! This may sound paradoxical because human beings tend to cherish their emotions and regard them as something specifically human, something which endows them with human qualities. In reality most of these emotions are of the same nature as those experienced by animals. They may be more complicated and sophisticated, but their essence is not fundamentally different from those of animals.

One of the essential tasks of the regression work is to unmask certain emotions which are not the product of samskaras and are beyond the range of animals. To distinguish these from the samskara-related emotions, the word 'feeling' will be used.

A crucial result of the regression process is to make us realise that, from morning to night, we tend to react to the world with stereotyped conditioning, just like Pavlov's dogs, instead of tapping from our human potential of 'creative being'. In terms of our four-fold model of subtle bodies, the essential difference between a human being and an animal is that the human being has gained a Higher Self. How much of your Higher Self is involved in your emotional responses? This is a key point, in which lies the answer to the question: which of our emotions are human and which are animal?

1.9 The story of King Janaka and the son of the ṛṣi

Let us conclude this chapter with a story from Sanskrit literature.

Once upon a time there was a great ṛṣi (seer-sage) of ancient India who sent his thirteen-year-old son to the court of King Janaka, and asked the prestigious sovereign to perfect the young boy's education. As soon as the boy arrived at the court, Janaka placed a jar of milk on his head. The jar was full to the brim, and Janaka instructed the boy to walk around the palace three times, without spilling one drop of milk.

The palace was full of rare statues and precious stones, full of jugglers, strange animals and beautiful women dancing – a lot of tempting things for a young man who had never left his father's ashram in the jungle before. Yet the son of the *ṛṣi* was able to see without reacting, and he went round the palace three times without spilling one single drop.

King Janaka was very pleased with the boy. He said to him, "Son, go back to your father and tell him there is nothing more I can teach you."

This certainly did not mean that the boy's emotional life was suppressed. But a certain form of reactional emotion had been eradicated. The boy could love, enjoy and feel, but his feelings were coming from within his soul, and were not sheer reactions to his environment. He could walk in the world and remain full inside, whatever surrounded him. He had worked out all his samskaras and was free, in the highest meaning of the word. Even the enlightened King Janaka, legendary for his wisdom, had nothing more to teach him.

CHAPTER 2

SAMSKARAS AND THE QUEST FOR FREEDOM

2.1 The tyranny of samskaras

If we are in quest of freedom, then it should be clear that our main hindrances are our own samskaras. There are circumstances in life that are limiting and restricting. If the price of oil rises, we cannot drive our cars as freely as we used to. If an administration asks us to fill out mountains of forms, then business becomes very difficult. But even in the most totalitarian country you will never find a dictatorship as restrictive and as permanent as that of the samskaras. Most people are concerned about dictatorships, yet who really cares about samskaras? This can help you to understand what both Hindus and Buddhists mean by *māyā*, or illusion. In Sanskrit, *māyā* means 'magic'. Samskaras operate an absolute and magic dictatorship about which no one even cares. The dictatorship starts before birth and does not stop with death. It obstructs your free will from morning to night, every single day spent on this planet. And you don't even see it – that is what is really magic about it.[1]

Consider again the example of the woman who was sexually assaulted when she was three years old, and who has totally lost any conscious recollection of the event. Can we really say that she is free

---

[1] The concept of the magic illusion of emotions is not only to be found in Hindu philosophy. The Christian mystic Gregory of Nyssa, for instance, used the word *gohteia*, magic, to describe 'the varied illusions' of this life, by which men are fooled, and which make them lose their own nature and behave like animals, as if they had drunk a beverage of Circe the sorceress. The same concept can also be found in Plotinus (Enn. iv,3,17). For a more detailed study, see Daniélou, Jean, *Platonisme et Théologie Mystique*, Ed. Montaigne, Paris, 1944, p. 126.

in her relationships with men? Seen from the outside, she is totally 'free'. Nobody forces her to choose such and such a man, and if she divorces four times it is entirely her responsibility. Yet knowing the terrible pressure exerted by the latent emotion, knowing the samskara and its dynamism, can we maintain the same assertion? The woman does not even know that her choices are being influenced by the samskara. Actually she does not even know that the samskara is imprinted; she may believe herself free while her emotional life is being manipulated by a force that she never sees. This is the first common scheme by which a samskara, an emotional imprint made in the past, can enslave you without you suspecting it.

However, this scheme needs to be extended, for when practising regression it becomes clear that people are not influenced only by samskaras from early childhood. Some of the samskaras which emerge cannot possibly be related to any circumstance of this present life. It is to be stressed again that it does not matter whether you believe in past lives or not. In reality, the fewer beliefs you have, the better; for beliefs generate expectations, and expectations in turn tend to distort the purity of the experience. The important point is that some samskaras are discovered that cannot possibly be related to this present life. Yet these samskaras prove crucial to understanding the likes and dislikes that govern your present choices and the way you manage your life. Let us look at a few examples which illustrate the main mechanisms by which samskaras interfere.

2.2 Superimposition

Case study – Mary was a twenty-four-year-old woman, going through a phase of intense depression. She got married when she was eighteen, but proved unable to remain true to her husband. She had a first lover after eighteen months of marriage, and then another one five months later, which broke up her marriage. Then she went to pieces. She started going from one man to another, multiplying short and superficial experiences that left her more and more devastated. Here is the narration of a key experience she had during one of her regressions.

What is the feeling now? – Cold. Terribly cold.

Cold inside or outside? –Both.

What does it look like around you? –It's damp. It's cold, cold, cold... made of stones. I can see this big building made of stones, and it is... terrible, worse than anything. It's so cold... I didn't want to come here. Or maybe I did, but now I don't want to be here anymore.

What is happening in this building? –It's a convent. I am locked in. I want to go away. It is horrid, as if the coldness outside was freezing my heart. Nobody cares. Nobody smiles. Sometimes I cry, but I am all alone. Sometimes I can't even cry, I am like dead...

Do you sometimes feel the same coldness in this present life? –Oh! yes. When I need somebody to care for me. Truly I just want warmth, and nothing else.

But this feeling, is it yours, or the one of the woman locked in the convent? –It is hers. It comes from her. But then it comes to me... it becomes mine.

Next time when it comes to you, could you recognise that it is *her* feeling, not yours? –Yes, that's quite clear.

This example is quite typical of a samskara of a remote past that interferes with one's daily life. Mary had never stayed in a convent during her present life. Yet since her childhood she had expressed some very mixed feelings as far as contemplative life was concerned. She was sometimes attracted, and sometimes terrified by it. Gradually, her being drawn to religious life became a joke to all her friends, who knew the promiscuous type of life she was leading.[1]

It is important to realise how Mary felt when she was alone in this present life. The terrible loneliness of the locked up nun *superimposed* itself upon her present emotional life. The feelings of this young woman here and now were a mixture of the past and the present, impossible to disentangle. This superimposed distress left her devastated, and ready to do anything so that someone would care for her. Yet seen from the outside, Mary was 'free' to run from one lover to another – which shows how one can be completely misled

---

[1] In regression, it is not rare to discover such patterns in which an ascetic life is followed by one with promiscuous sexual activity and indulging in sensual experiences.

when judging somebody according to so-called moral principles. As soon as the underlying samskara was recognised through regression, the suffering of this woman could never be as intense as before.

Case study – Samantha, aged twenty-five. The beginning of the ISIS session revealed a painful spot in the area of the ribcage. Samantha started feeling very distressed and breathing quickly, as if out of breath. She looked as if she was suffering considerably.

What are you feeling now? –Fear. I am being hurt. My head and my back are being kicked. [She was sobbing and panting, curling up on the mattress, as if she was trying to escape from blows.]
Can you move? –I can only try to protect myself.
Why are they doing that? –Because I am easy to kick around.
Does it feel like being rather young, or old? –Pretty young. Male.
Does it last for a long time? –For a while. And then they leave me in the dust and run away laughing. They were young... about my age.
And then? –Anger. Frustration. Humiliation. [Still sobbing.]
Do you sometimes get the same emotion in your [present] life? –Yes, same feeling.
Is there anybody around? –No. That was outside the village.
What does the village look like? –Small. Dirt roads. Most of the houses are flat-topped. Dirt.
Any trees? –No. It is very dry and warm. There is an Arabic-Muslim sort of feeling about the village. [The client was still out of breath.]
Are there also some good people in the village? –My mother. I do not have any friends. I can see my father sitting there, drinking coffee. He does not talk to me much. I feel about twelve or fourteen years old. Sometimes I have to support my arm. It looks withered, it is not as big as the other one.
Can it move? –A little bit. [For the rest of the session, the client kept massaging her right arm.]
Are the legs okay? –Okay, but I'm not very strong. I'm tall.
What happened to this arm? –It's always been like this, ever since I was small. I can't do much with it.
What do you do after you've been beaten? –I just get up and walk. I walk, I go away from the village. I just walk for hours. I feel so

20

hopeless, humiliated. [Crying.] What can I do? I just want to go away.

And then where do you go? –There is nowhere I can go, I have to go back to the village. I know it is going to happen again, because it always does. I can't talk to my father, because he thinks I should stand up for myself. I go to my mother, but there is nothing she can do. She just comforts me as much as possible. I keep on thinking all the time that I wish I were born stronger. I wish I could defend myself... How weak I am. I don't like myself.

Do you sometimes feel like this in your [present Australian] life? –Yes, same feeling that I can't stand up for myself.

Does the boy have any friends? –No. I'm not like the others, I am ashamed and they stay away. And they make fun of me.

Do you also feel that, in your [present] life? –Yes, I alienate myself, pulling away from people. Not feeling good enough and therefore not risking the chance of being made fun of.

Can you feel that this emotion is not really yours, but that it is the emotion of the boy? –Yes. It is his vibration.

And then? –I am in a street. There are donkeys. No cars, but carts pulled by donkeys. Whenever I am in the street there are always comments. People gossip behind my back. It's a pretty miserable life. I do some work on the land, but it doesn't matter what I do, I just think about how I am. I feel defeated. I wake up in the morning, I walk, I work on this land, I walk back, and it is all I have. I'm wearing a turban. I'm very tall.

[Later in the session, the client came to reexperience the death of the crippled man.] –I seem to be lying down. It feels as though I'm dying in my sleep. I am lifting. Something is going out through my head. I am going up. Then I have the feeling of meeting my mother, as if she had been waiting for me. There is a sense of relief. And then, after some time, I get this blackness. Everything disappears in the blackness.

This is a perfect example of how a samskara is carried on from one life to another. One can understand why the crippled young Arabic man felt alienated and insecure. Of course, one can be crippled and extremely enlightened and happy. But at least the despair of the

21

Arabic boy had some tangible foundation. It was not necessary but it was understandable.

Yet, Samantha does not suffer from any illness or infirmity. When she withdraws from possible friendships, when she feels inhibited and rejected in life, due to the *same* emotions, then it becomes absurd and mind-boggling. **The crippled arm has long since disappeared, yet the accompanying emotion has carried on.** The emotional pattern of the cripple has been superimposed on Samantha's emotions since her childhood, without her noticing it.

Absurd? Indeed! Yet it is exactly how we are functioning, constantly. Modalities and intensity may vary, but it is always the same scheme. An inappropriate pattern gets impressed deep inside, and it persists long after its generating cause has disappeared. "I am no longer locked in a convent, yet I keep on behaving as if I wanted to be comforted at any cost", or "I no longer have a crippled arm, nor do I live in a society that would reject me if I had one. Yet I still feel alienated and left out." These emotions are sheer reflections from the past. They are illusory and unreal in the sense that they do not rest on anything tangible, but, at the same time, the suffering and the mess they create in our minds and in our lives are extremely real.

2.3 Endless repetitions

Case study – Thirty-year-old woman.

What are you feeling? –I can see the house. It is made of light material. The colours are really different. I've never seen colours like these before.[1] There are many more yellow and orange hues. A

---

[1] In regression, it is not rare for clients to reexperience episodes in which colours appear different from those that are usually perceived. This could be due to the fact that each time we incarnate in a new body, we get slightly different eyesight, which transmits different colour signals to our mind. Another possibility is that the general perception of colours of the whole of mankind has evolved with time. Many observations have led me to opt for the second possibility – even though the first one could also play some part. In episodes taking place from the 19th and 20th century onwards, colours and images appear 'flatter' and less endowed with perspective and dimension. As well, episodes taking place before the 19th century often con-

beautiful woman with long dark hair. She looks Japanese. She is standing at the door, looking outside.

What is she doing? –Her husband has gone, he's left her. And her life stops there. She knows that she will never see him again. It's finished. It is not even pain, it is worse than that. She is shattered. She just stops functioning.

In this regression a major samskara of being abandoned is unveiled. In her present life, whenever this woman was abandoned by a man, her suffering was unbearable, because the distress of the Japanese woman superimposed on her 'own' reactions. Her pain took place on two levels, but she could not see that until she went through the regression process. Whatever can't be seen is ten times more painful, because there is no way one can understand it. Being abandoned was for her like falling into a bottomless pit, caught in suffering beyond any possibility of rationalisation.

A crucial detail is that the client, in this present life, had chosen a husband who travelled a lot. Each time the man went away, the couple managed to have a terrible fight, so that each departure had a taste of final separation, and the woman would reexperience the throes of being abandoned. Instead of saying to herself "We had a good fight because I hate to see him go, but anyway he'll be back in two months", she would become desperate, like the Japanese woman. And the same drama was replayed twice a year.

This tendency to always repeat the same ordeal is the direct product of the dynamism of samskaras. The emotional wound of the samskara is too painful, it cannot remain neutral. It is crying out to be healed. The emotional charge associated with the samskara is so intense that as long as you don't deal with it, it tends to generate circumstances that allow it to express itself. In many cases, this will result in replaying similar circumstances, from life to life.

---

vey the feeling of a much greater variety of colours and hues, and the colours appear more 'alive'. It is as if something had 'shrunk' in our perception of colours around the 19th century. If we go even further back in time, before the Atlantean flood, we discover colours that are more akin to our present peripheral vision at night, and quite similar to the basic hue of astral light.

After having seen how samskaras tend to superimpose emotional reactions on top of your present consciousness, we are now introducing a second major mechanism. Samskaras tend to make you create life circumstances through which they can manifest. They not only magnify your present pain and emotions by superimposition, they manipulate you to create difficulties in which the emotions can be replayed. They act like latent tendencies, heavily influencing your destiny.

2.4 Māyā, illusion

Until now, we have only considered the big animals in the jungle of samskaras – those major emotional traumas created by dramatic circumstances. If we want to get a clear picture of how the mind functions, we must take into account many other little traces left by experiences that were not so intense. Yet these traces have persisted and keep on 'bugging' your present perception of the world.

Let us take an example. You walk into a friend's kitchen, and there is a particular smell in the air. Immediately this smell reminds you of a kitchen where you spent part of your childhood. In this kitchen there was a cat sleeping under the table, and there was an old lady working. All sorts of memories flash back into your mind. If you were feeling good in that kitchen, the good feeling comes back to you while you are in your friend's kitchen. So, maybe you are going to feel comfortable and tell your friend "I like your kitchen!"

Now, suppose you were feeling extremely uncomfortable with the old lady, because she used to force you to eat artichokes, which you hated. And on this particular day your friend happens to be cooking artichokes. The malaise will be remembered – the anxiety in your chest, the tension in your belly. You are not really feeling anxious and tense, but the memories are vivid. By the way, you are completely split off from your friend's kitchen while the recollections take place. If the friend is talking to you during this time, you may well have to ask him to repeat what he just said. You have been abducted by this past episode.

This example assumes that you could consciously remember the episode during which the samskara had been imprinted. Suppose now that you have completely forgotten all about the old lady's kitchen. Something different is likely to happen. You walk into your friend's place, the general atmosphere and the smell trigger an unconscious connection with the forgotten episode, and a certain malaise ensues. There is some degree of anxiety in your chest and tension in your belly, *and you do not know why*. You do not remember any of the actual details of the old lady's kitchen, there is just the malaise. The emotional package of the past is superimposing itself on your present consciousness, through the link of the smell – but you do not perceive this. You are only aware of two things: the kitchen and your discomfort. So you may well think, "I don't like the vibrations in this house!", or "I don't feel comfortable with these people". Of course, the kitchen is exactly the same, it is only your perception that has changed. So your judgment is completely irrelevant and absurd. Yet all this comes to your mind very 'naturally' and 'logically'.

While you are being caught in this mode of reaction, you may think that what you are seeing is your friend's kitchen. But you are completely fooling yourself. You are seeing *your* kitchen, full of unconscious projections of artichoke-ghosts, and what your friend is seeing of his kitchen is completely different. *Your* kitchen has nothing to do with the real kitchen, it is nothing more than a construction of your mind. At that moment you are disconnected; you are living in an imaginary world as if in a cage; you are anywhere but 'here and now'. Your judgment is impaired by an unseen factor, and any major decision that you might have to take in this kitchen is likely to be distorted and lead you astray.

The next step is to see that such superimpositions take place constantly, not only throughout the day, but even during your dreams! A simple example of superimposition that many people have consciously experienced is that of songs or pieces of music they used to listen to in a certain period of their life. If the same music is heard some years later, then the 'flavour', the atmosphere and the feelings of that particular period immediately flash back to their consciousness.

Whether you are aware of it or not, the situation is such that innumerable similar recollections are constantly clouding your present perception of the world. Quite often, several samskaras are triggered simultaneously, each superimposing its own package of emotions and impressions, which adds to the confusion. Imagine your friend in his kitchen playing the song you used to listen to ten years ago, when you had a broken heart, or perhaps when you received the best news of your life... what a jam! Many minor samskaras are not associated with a clear emotion, but just with a vague feeling of malaise or elation. When activated, they just superimpose a little attraction or repulsion, an indistinct blurriness on top of your present perception.

If we sum up the influences of all the jumbo-samskaras, the medium-sized and the micro ones, we can get a picture of what *māyā* (illusion) is. There is absolutely no need to deny the physical reality of the world to come to the conclusion that we live in a complete *māyā*, or illusion. Whether the universe is real or not is not the problem at this stage, for we are not living in the universe – we are living in our samskara-world. We *never* see our friend's kitchen, or anybody else's kitchen; we only catch a strange and unclear mixture of the room itself and of our own projections. We *never* see the tree around the corner, because it is like another tree we bumped into some years ago and some unconscious tension surfaces each time we approach it. We *never* see our friends the way they really are because the way they talk, the way they dress, the way they present themselves presses our buttons and makes us project impressions and images onto them. These impressions have more to do with our pool of samskaras than with who our friends really are. Between our conscious memories and our unconscious superimpositions, we do not see the world, we dream it.

Hindu masters often like to emphasise the dramatic character of this situation. We spend our time getting upset at the dramas of our life, but all these dramas are but trifles compared to the tragedy of being permanently isolated in a samskara-generated cloud of illusion – a cage. We never see the world, we can only see *our* world, which is full of the ghosts of our past. We are disconnected, living in a cloud, and we do not even suspect it. Right from the beginning, it should be made very clear that the purpose of a genuine work of regression is gradually to dispel this cloud of illusion, not to indulge in following the stories of our past.

2.5 *Likes and dislikes*

When you are in quest of your Self, it is always valuable to ponder on what in yourself feels central and essential – the core of your 'me'. In this respect, it is interesting to look at the roots of your likes and dislikes. It is a fact that many people tend to consider their tastes and attractions as quite a central part of their personality. Some people have a special affinity with a certain colour, for instance, and choose all their clothes accordingly. If they walk into a place with the same colour on the walls, they immediately feel, "That's my colour, that's a place for me." Whether it has to do with colours, food or anything else, people often tend to look to their likes and dislikes when they seek to define themselves, to apprehend what is their 'me', as opposed to 'non-me'.

Case study – Twenty-five-year-old man.

What are you feeling now? –Pain, pain, pain... always pain. It never ends.

How does your body feel, big, or small? –Big. It's a big man. He's got huge shoulders. [Laughing:] I feel like a shrimp compared to him. [Then the pain gets worse and the young man is nearly screaming.] This will never end, this will never end!

Does it feel like being indoors or outdoors? –Indoors. It's dark. It's underground. It's a little room and it's cold. Pain, pain, pain... they're torturing me and it never ends.

What kind of emotion goes with that? –Hatred. If only I could move from that table, I would kill the three of them, absolutely nothing could stop me. But I'm tightly chained, and it goes on and on. One of them is reciting verses in Latin. [Yelling:] They're cutting through my chest!

This hatred, have you ever felt it in this present life? –Yes, unexpectedly, I've always hated Latin! When I was at school I had this passionate hatred for Latin, without any real reason. I had such a contempt for the Latin teacher, I was always trying to be awful to her... It's not Latin, it's them! I could kill them, and the other hypocrite who is reciting his Latin verses while they are torturing me. Oh!

Lord! Oh! Lord! It's like I'm turning towards God with all the forces I've got left. Oh Lord! Will it never end?
[The quality of vibration changes in the room, as if an angel had appeared; the client can hardly speak.] –There is a white light that's coming down. It's massive. I'm out. I'm not in my body any more. I can see what they are trying to do to my body from above. It doesn't matter any more. Now there is only the light.

A regression process invites you to reconsider many of your attractions and dislikes, and to discover whether they correspond to real aspirations of your Higher Self or whether they are nothing other than the mechanical result of samskaric imprints. In this respect, regression can be regarded as a path of de-conditioning.

However, it must be stressed that this path has little, if anything, to do with 'renouncing your desires'. When people try to renounce their desires, in the great majority of cases they end up suppressing them. Conceptually, there is something wrong in trying to condition oneself not to have a desire. Suppose the desire is itself coming from the conditioning of a samskara; it can't be satisfying to try to add another conditioning on top of the conditioning. **The aim of ISIS is de-conditioning.** The only thing ISIS asks you to do is to look systematically for the source of your reactions, including your attractions and dislikes. It may appear that a number of attractions and dislikes are obviously the result of the influence of samskaras, in which case they are likely to fall by themselves once the samskara has been released. That happens by itself, and has nothing painful associated with it. It is more like getting rid of an artificial burden than anything else. The end result of the process is not a wishy-washy desire-free condition, but a mature state in which one's genuine spontaneity has been unveiled and one's true purpose has been found, beyond all conditioning.

Case study – Forty-three-year-old woman.

What can you perceive now? –They're going to kill him. They've taken him away. It is breaking my heart. I never even had the time to tell this man how I loved him. And now it's too late. He will be executed tomorrow, and no one can do anything about it. I'll never see him again... [wave of despair].

Is there any correspondence between this episode and any event in your present life? –Once I fell madly in love with a man who had exactly the same eyes. It was an impossible situation. He was married, and I was married. For months I could not get him out of my mind. It was the same broken heart. It took me one year to recover.

It is essential to understand that when such a 'love-at-first-sight' connection takes place between two people, it should not necessarily be inferred that they have already met in a former life. This point can never be emphasized enough, because it will save some romantic souls from making enormous mistakes and justifying them through the practice of regression.

Remember the fantastic computer in *The Hitch-Hikers' Guide to the Galaxy*? You feed the computer with the decision you have made, and it immediately comes out with a list of brilliant reasons to explain why your decision is the only one that makes sense. Interestingly, some people try to do exactly the same with regression. They have already made up their mind that they want to start a new relationship or get rid of their partner, and they try regression to find a past-life reason to comfort them in their decision. They want to believe that destiny is at play, instead of owning their choice. They want regression to show that their new partner is a soul mate with whom they have already been associated in former lives. But, unless the connector is ready to lull them like the galactic hitch-hikers' computer, what they end up finding is usually of quite a different nature.

Past-life connections do exist, but they do not necessarily manifest in the form of magnetic attractions. Actually, in most cases when such an attraction takes place, it has nothing to do with a past-life connection. If we take the last regression, what do we find? The client has met a man who had eyes similar to those of someone she was passionately in love with in a former life. This, along with a few other similarities, has triggered a huge samskara which reactivated the pain she felt when losing the other man in the past life. This is where one has to be very careful. The intensity of the emotion only indicates that a big samskara is triggered, and is in no way a sign of a past-life connection. Usually, the louder the emotion in your psyche, the more likely its source is a samskara.

It may be painful to realise that the same passionate attraction could happen with any other person who, for one reason or another, happens to trigger the same samskara. Yet, this realisation could save you a lot of time and wandering, for relationships based on samskaras are far from being the most fulfilling or the most durable. The layer of samskaras is comparable to a kaleidoscope. Its polarities, attractions and repulsions are perpetually moving and changing under the influence of a myriad of irrational micro-factors.

Let this be clear, I am not suggesting that it is only due to samskaras that people fall in love – just as regression does not imply that all affective waves in a human being are due to samskaras. Regression teaches us that when a samskara is activated, we are manipulated. We may believe that we are making decisions from our own free will, but in reality it is the samskara that projects us in one direction or another. It is nothing other than a prerecorded reaction – a conditioning that is triggered and that compels us to move in a certain direction (unless we become aware of what is going on). Then, sooner or later, the kaleidoscope rotates a little and the attraction falls flat. We end up not understanding what we are doing with such a partner, or in such a job, or in any other situation where we have put ourselves under the magic spell of the samskara.

CHAPTER 3

EMOTIONS VERSUS FEELINGS

3.1 The love of the cat and the love of Christ

In English, the word 'love' can be used in quite different contexts. For instance, when the cat comes and shows affection just before you feed it, you easily say that the cat loves you. If you are sensitive enough to know how to talk with cats, you can even hear the cat whispering, "I love you. You are such a nice person. You are so smart, for a human." Obviously the cat loves you.

The same word, love, is also used to describe what emanates from Christ, or from enlightened masters or guides, when they give all of themselves to a disciple. Some of these masters have an incredible capacity for love. Love radiates from them like a breathtaking force; you can feel it 'physically'. Close to them, it is as if you were bathing in an ocean of sweetness. All sorrow, frustration and violence in you are softened. Obviously the guide loves you.

However, the love of Christ and the love of the cat are of a very different order. For instance, kick the cat out of the house instead of feeding it dinner. Instantly, the cat no longer loves you. It hisses. If you can speak cat, you hear something like, "I hate you! Sooner or later I'll kill you!" Now, if you kick Christ out of your house, that is not going to change His love at all. The love of Christ does not depend on your feedback. It is unconditional. It takes place on a completely different level from the conditional tokens of affection of the cat. Yet we use the same word, love, for both cat and Christ.

In the same manner, the word 'emotion' is used to qualify psychological tendencies or forces of completely different essences. This does not apply only to English but to modern languages in gen-

31

eral. The irascibility of a driver blocked in a traffic jam, the lust or the jealousy of a lover, the fear of death, the anxiety that precedes an exam, the compassion of an enlightened Buddha, the anger of a little child, the aesthetic feeling that arises when admiring the beauty of a landscape, the exalted inner wave of a saint in communion with divinity – all these are labelled with the same word, emotion, regardless of the fact that they take place in very different spheres of ourselves. This shows that an enormous amount of confusion has arisen in our world as far as emotions are concerned.

3.2 Emotions and samskaras

A great secret of wisdom is: to know something, find its source. This can be applied to a whole range of spiritual mysteries, including our present topic. In order to learn to discriminate between the various kinds of emotions, it is essential to find their sources. Different emotions come from very different parts of yourself, which will give clues as to what to do with them.

One of the principal characteristics of samskaras is that they tend to generate emotions. An imprint, or samskara, is left by an experience. When a related experience takes place, an emotion is triggered. For instance, you have had a bad car accident somewhere in town. After that, every time you drive past the same place, an emotion arises inside you. The dramatic circumstances of the accident are recalled and a reaction takes place. Fear, anxiety, or some level of discomfort is experienced. Three elements can be discerned in this emotional response:

    –the stimulus (driving past the same place);
    –the samskara (the emotional imprint left by the accident);
    –the reactional emotion (anxiety, discomfort).
We can summarise the sequence:

---

stimulus ➜ samskara ➜ reactional emotion

The stimulus triggers the samskara, and a reactional emotion takes place. At least there is not much doubt as to the nature of this emotion; it comes from conditioning. The emotion is like a stereotyped routine of the mind; it is highly predictable. Each time you drive past the place, the reacting mind plays its prerecorded message. It will not be difficult for you to transpose the analysis of this mechanism to your own life and find a whole range of similar emotions that can be traced back to certain traumatic events.

This type of emotion will not foster inner clarity. It is more like a wrong chemical reaction that takes place each time the samskara is triggered. There is something sick about it. It is like a wound which calls for healing. Moreover, it obviously does not arise from the spontaneity of your soul; it is sheer conditioning. The emotional response does not originate from your true Self. It is nothing more than a prerecorded message that is repeated each time the right stimulus is met.

The problem is that you are often unaware of these mechanisms at work inside yourself. Ninety-nine percent of the time, you miss them completely. Remember the examples of samskaras developed in previous chapters. It was only after going through the exploration process of regression that the clients could see that their emotions originated from samskaras. If you have lost any conscious memory of the samskara, it is highly probable that you will miss the connection. An emotion will spring up into your field of consciousness, triggered by a stimulus, and the same sequence will take place:

stimulus → samskara → emotion

However, if the samskara has been buried in the depths of your unconscious, what will you perceive? The stimulus, the emotion, and nothing else. As far as your perception is concerned, the sequence has been shortened into:

stimulus → emotion

For example, someone says a few words to you and a response comes immediately, in words or in thoughts, "I like this person" or "This person is stupid", depending on the content of the stimulus. Or you are driving and you hear the driver behind you honking, and then you hear yourself answering with an insult. But the middle element – the key link – is missed. You are completely unaware of the samskara that makes you react to the stimulus. You have been tricked. You may think "I responded", but truly there is nothing of your Self in that response. It is just another prerecorded message that is played automatically once the appropriate button has been pressed.

Extend this model to the myriads of samskaras hidden in your mind: those you know, and those you do not even suspect exist, but are still active. It becomes obvious that a large proportion of your emotions, in all aspects of your life, from the most minute to the most intense, can be related to this sequence: stimulus → samskara → emotion. This pattern is too mechanical – too puppet-like to satisfy the aspiration of the Spirit. Yet the bitter fact is that most of your emotions are reactions to a stimulus that triggers a samskara of some sort.

Most, but not all. From time to time, a light arises in the heart, and a different 'frequency of being' is experienced. An emotion comes that is not the screaming expression of a pressing demand and that does not come from the mechanical stimulation of a samskara.

In a genuine quest for freedom, part of the work must be aimed at de-conditioning. Rediscovering spontaneity implies that you can separate Being from its facade, true emotions from conditioned ones, and expressions of the Self from reactions of the samskaras.

3.3 Emotions versus feelings

At this stage, we need to introduce two different words for emotions: one for those related to the affection shown by the cat, and one for those akin to the unconditional love of Christ. For the conditional ones, I will use the word 'emotions'. For the unconditional ones, I will use the word 'feelings'.

Some other words might have been chosen. However, the etymology of the word 'emotion' fits quite well with the use that is suggested here. Motion means movement. The prefix 'e-' is a shortened form of 'ex-', indicating a movement towards the outside, as in exit or excrete. E-motion means 'movement outside' and emotions, precisely, take you out of yourself. They come from the layer of samskaras and not from the Self. They make you respond in a way that does not involve your Self, but is just a mechanical reaction in the layer of samskaras (astral body). E-motions make you wander far from your real nature.

The word 'feeling' has the advantage of being used by both Rudolf Steiner and Hindu masters of Vedanta, with the same meaning of 'knowledge by identity' as will be developed in this book. Thus our vocabulary is consistent with as many sources as possible.

3.4 Emotion and reaction

An essential criterion to discern an emotion from a feeling is that the emotion is a reaction, whereas the feeling is not. From this perspective, the terms 'emotion' and 'reactional emotion' are therefore synonymous.

The word 'reaction' is extremely appropriate, for it has connotations in the fields of chemistry and physics, that is, the mechanical functioning of the world. Think of a chemical reaction. For instance, put a block of metallic sodium into water, and an explosion ensues. Or mix hydrochloric acid and liquid ammonia, and a spectacular cloud of white smoke is released. A given cocktail of physical causes always creates the same effect.

Even though emotions may appear more complex due to the fluidity of the psychological field, they can be related to a similar pattern. A stimulus comes from the outer world; it triggers a samskara; and an emotional response automatically follows. For example, in the days of the Cold War, some people would get angry each time they heard 'communism'. It worked like a charm every time the word was uttered in their presence. Other people would get angry each time they heard 'anticommunism', with just as much consistency. Even if they did not show their emotion overtly, you could see that something inside them was reacting. They thought themselves very different from the former group, but in terms of samskaras was there really so much difference?

Emotions are not only mechanical, but also 'physiological' and even 'chemical'. This can be illustrated with a simple but striking experiment – borrow a stethoscope, and listen to your intestines. Place the flat end of the stethoscope on the skin, somewhere around your navel or in the right iliac area. Listen to the natural sound that comes from the unceasing motion of your digestive tract. Next, think of something unpleasant, such as somebody you dislike, or something that frightens you, or that makes you feel uncomfortable. Immediately the sound of your intestines changes! As your ear gets more accustomed to listening through the stethoscope, you realise that the change is far from minor. The sound suddenly becomes

35

much more rough and scrappy, incredibly disharmonious. Obviously this unpleasant little thought is sufficient to completely modify the functioning of your bowels, the movement of its muscle fibres, and consequently the chemistry of digestion. Listen for yourself. How could a proper digestion process take place with such a sound! You will easily come to the conclusion that there must be some literal truth to the statement, "poisoned by your emotions".

3.5 Emotions can always turn into their opposite

A major drawback of emotions is that their magic is transient and changing. If you have been attracted to a certain person or a certain professional occupation due to the wind of a samskara, it is quite likely that sooner or later you will get disenchanted, lose interest, and be attracted elsewhere. Another stimulus will trigger another samskara, and all former resolutions will fall flat. Samskaras operate in your mind like a kaleidoscope. Just a little movement, and a completely different configuration appears. The world was green, and suddenly it appears pink. In reality the world has not changed at all, but it only takes a fraction of a second for you to see it totally differently when looking through the kaleidoscopic goggles of the samskaras.

A good way to know if your love pertains to emotions or to feelings is to ask yourself what would happen if you were rejected, or betrayed. A love which is an emotion can easily turn into its opposite. In one second, "You see your friend as a pig covered in filth, as a chariot full of devils".[1] If your love is akin to feeling, then it will not be stopped by a negative response on the part of the beloved. The criterion is a bitter one, but if it is applied with sincerity it may save you a lot of self-delusion and wandering.

3.6 The one thousand masks of emotions

Anger, rage, frustration, irritation, despair, sadness, depression – all these can be listed as emotions. Nobody will complain about a system that allows you to get rid of them. Later on, it may appear that you are much more attached to these emotions than you thought in the beginning, and that you actually cherish them as treasures.

---

[1] I-Ching, hexagram 38, 'Opposition', sixth mutable line.

Yet, whatever meandering you may have to go through, the intellect is not shocked by the idea of getting rid of anger or depression.

However, if you start observing your reactions in a systematic manner, it will become obvious that the pattern 'stimulus → samskara → emotion' does not only apply to anger and depression, but also to a number of so-called 'positive emotions'. In many cases, when you display love, charity, compassion or various forms of moral behaviour, it is the same sequence which is involved.

To put it simply, you realise that most of the time your love is similar to the love of the cat. You give as long as you are fed. Of course, you are not asking for exactly the same things as the cat. You want to hear or feel that you are beautiful, or something equivalent that comforts you and makes you feel safe. But the basic pattern is the same – if you are kicked out, your emotion is immediately modified, or even turns into its opposite.

The realisation is indeed challenging. It calls unequivocally for a reorientation of values. If 'good' actions can spring from the puppet-like level of the samskaras, then what truly is good or bad? A stale sense of the moral cliches of good and bad emerges. These become inadequate to apprehend the reality of emotions and feelings.

CHAPTER 4

THE CAUSALITY OF EMOTIONS AND FEELINGS

4.1 Emotions and thought processes

The distinctions we have made between emotions and feelings can also be applied to different forms of thoughts. Many thoughts are akin to emotions in the sense that they are nothing more than reactions. Understanding this point will lead us to a broader definition of emotions.

Try the following experiment. Sit down quietly and start watching your thoughts. Don't try to stop them. Don't interfere with them in any way. Just become aware of them as they arise in your mind. This, by itself, is a major technique of meditation. In the beginning you cannot discern much because the mind is too quick; the thoughts follow one another uninterruptedly, and you end up 'thinking' instead of meditating. As you keep on practising, however, the mind tends to slow down, and you become able to see each thought as soon as it appears in your field of consciousness. At this point you can make an essential observation. If you can just watch the thought without any form of reaction, it fades away. Then another thought comes up. Repeat the same process. Look at it without reacting to it, and the thought passes away. If you could maintain this attitude, watching without reacting, your peace of mind would be permanently established, for the thoughts would be like birds flying in the background of a landscape.[1] They wouldn't disturb you much and they wouldn't leave any trace in your mind.

But it is not so. Each time a thought or a perception arises, the tendency of the mind is to grasp it, and to chain another thought to it

---

[1] An analogy taken from Sri Aurobindo.

through some kind of association. For example, you hear a noise coming from your fridge, and the mind says, "The fridge is empty". Then it follows with "Brünnhilde is coming for lunch" and "I have to go shopping", "But first I have to go to the bank", and so on. Or a thought arises about your friend Victor, and the mind goes on "He is not as nice as Zacharias", and then "Zacharias owes me some money", and "How could I remind him politely?", and so the endless dance goes on.

It should be clear that this *modus operandi* is fundamentally similar to the pattern we have described for emotions.

stimulus → samskara → reaction

In the case of thinking, the stimulus is the first thought, such as Victor, or a sense perception, such as the noise of the fridge. The reaction is the following thought that the mind grasps and links onto it. Then the second thought in turn becomes a stimulus for the following reaction, and so on:

thought or perception → micro-samskara → another thought

However, if there was not a micro-samskara making an association between every two thoughts, the mind would simply stop and become silent. These samskaras may not be endowed with as much emotional charge as those we have considered so far, but still they have all the fundamental characteristics of samskaras. They are imprints in the mental substance which create a certain reaction when triggered by the right stimulus.

This approach sheds a different light on the unceasing stream of thoughts experienced when you close your eyes and watch your mind. These thoughts are nothing other than the result of the dynamism of your samskaras. If you no longer had samskaras, or if you could switch off the layer of samskaras, then when closing your eyes you would be able to stop thinking and go straight into higher realms of consciousness.

In Sanskrit, all the thoughts and little mental movements that continually take place in the mind are called *vrttis*. The root of the word, *vrt*, means 'to turn'. In the seminal text of the system of yoga, the *Yoga-Sūtras* of Patañjali, the very first instruction is, *yogas citta-vrtti-nirodah* (1.2), meaning "Yoga is the eradication of the *vṛttis* of the mind". The message is clear – as long as samskaras pollute your consciousness with constant reactional mental movements and emotions, the state of yoga, or transcendental unity, cannot be achieved. In Sanskrit, the layer in which all these reactions take place and in which the samskaras are embedded is called manas (corresponding to the astral body of the system of subtle bodies used in Clairvision work). Manas is usually translated into English as 'mind' and as we have seen, it is in this sense that the word 'mind' is used in this book.

It does not matter whether you perceive what comes from this manas/mind layer as thoughts, emotions, or a mixture of both. Whether thoughts or emotions, all of these are fundamentally reactions, triggered by samskaras. Their nature is akin to conditioned responses.

From this point of view, the problem is not so much to discern between thoughts and emotions, but to **discern between what is reaction and what is not**, what comes from samskaras and what does not. In other words, you want to be able to discriminate between the puppet-like mechanisms of the samskaras and the spontaneity of the Self. For this purpose, just as we have established a distinction between emotions and feelings, a clear distinction has to be made between those thoughts which originate from samskaras and those which do not.

The aim of this work is not to erase any form of thinking and turn you into a thought-free vegetable. Nevertheless, just as the emotions of the reacting mind can be gradually replaced by spontaneous feelings, so the thinking of the reacting mind can be replaced by the living thought of the transformed mind, or 'supermind' (transformed astral body). In order to have a clearer view of these transformations, we need to understand what feelings are about.

4.2 Feelings

If there was no princess, who would bother to fight the dragon? If the purpose was only to reach a certain emotional tranquillity, why should anybody engage in the long and difficult process of neutralising the manas/mind? It would be much simpler to learn to replace negative emotions with 'positive' ones, as with those methods where people are taught to send positive affirmations into the subconscious parts of their mind. Such practices can bring definite improvements. Conceptually, however, there is a weak point to them – they pile conditioning on top of conditioning. The depths of the mind are found to be repeating "I'm ugly and sick, I'm ugly and sick", so one covers them with "I'm beautiful, I'm beautiful", hoping that the mind will start repeating the latter even more than the former. These methods may help you become more successful in your daily routines, but they do not bring a resolution of the real problem – the eclipse of the Self caused by the samskaras. Positive affirmations may soothe the dragon, but they miss the princess. If our purpose is metaphysical freedom, we have to step out of the layer of the samskaras altogether, not replace a dark conditioning with a rosy one.

It is easy to talk about emotions, precisely because they belong to the manas/mind, and because our language mainly takes place in that layer. It is not so easy to talk about feelings, because by nature they transcend this layer. Feelings belong to the 'non-mind' (transformed astral body). Words can only give you an idea about feelings. But a mental idea about what is beyond the realm of the mind will never be a real understanding. Direct experience is needed.

The causality of feelings is completely different from that of emotions. Emotions often appear stupid, yet they follow a certain logic and are highly predictable. By contrast, feelings are beyond the realm of rational logic. For a long time, during your process of development, you never know in advance when a real feeling is going to take place. Feelings are like a gift, and the manas/mind has no control over them. It can block them, to a certain extent, but it cannot make them up.

It was said before that emotions can be perceived as waves. Feelings also can be described as inner waves, but of a completely different nature. Instead of taking you away from your centre, feelings reveal more of your Higher Self. They throw light on the true core of your personality. Instead of the superficial trepidation of emotions, a feeling is a deep and motionless awakening. Instead of an e-motion (movement outside), the feeling is an 'in-motion-lessness', a still wave that creates contact with the deeper parts of yourself. The direction of feelings is definitely centripetal, whereas that of emotions is centrifugal. Emotions scatter, they disperse your life in all directions; feelings centre.

Another characteristic of feelings is their density, or fullness. On the level of experience, emotions appear empty compared to the plenitude and the completeness of feelings. People who think that their life would be boring without the thrill of emotions have no idea what is on the other side of the manas/mind. Emotions create a tremulous agitation which remains confined within a thin layer. A feeling, on the other hand, is a multi-dimensional awakening, through which a fullness of being is experienced. You *are* more through feeling, whereas emotions steal away some of your being.

4.3 Emotions make you bypass the Self

The most essential difference between emotions and feelings is that emotions make you bypass the Self, or Higher Ego, while feelings are associated with it. To clarify this, let us use a simple model of subtle bodies. A human being can be regarded as made of:

1) a physical body;

2) an etheric body, or layer of life force, or envelope of prana;

3) an astral body, which corresponds to the manas/mind of the Hindu tradition, and which is the seat of emotions as well as of the thoughts that result from samskaras. Strictly speaking, the astral body is the structure, and the manas/mind is its function. The two cannot really be separated, and so the terms 'astral body' and 'manas/mind' can virtually be regarded as synonymous;[1]

4) a layer of Self-awareness that we call Ego, or Higher Ego, or Self, or Higher Self, or Spirit.

In this context, the meaning of the word Ego is quite different from that which is used by Hindu or Buddhist masters. To them the word ego refers to the 'little ego', or 'grasping ego' – the condition-

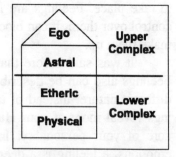

---

[1] The astral body not only encompasses the conscious mind, but also the subconscious and unconscious parts of the mind. Under normal circumstances, the vast majority of human beings are unaware and unconscious of most of the material stored in their astral body.

ing which is the product of samskaras. This 'little ego' is virtually synonymous with manas/mind, the layer of reactional emotions and conditioning, which corresponds to the astral body of our classification. For the purpose of simplicity, in the context of this book, as in *Awakening the Third Eye* and *Entities...*, the terms Ego, Higher Ego, Self, Higher Self and Spirit are used synonymously.

In terms of this model of four vehicles, the work of self-transformation can be described as a purification of the astral body, or manas/mind, following which the Self can be experienced in its purity and totality. Let us return to Patañjali's *Yoga-Sūtras*. As we saw, this handbook on enlightenment begins with, *yogaś citta-vṛtti-nirodaḥ*, "Yoga is the suppression of the fluctuations of *chitta*" (1.2). We certainly did not go astray by translating, "Yoga is the suppression of the fluctuations of the manas/mind", for *chitta* is nothing other than the 'substance' of the manas/mind. A more accurate rendering is therefore "Yoga is the eradication of the *vṛttis* from the substance of the mind". The next verse of the *Yoga-Sūtras* is:

tadā draṣṭuḥ svarūpe 'vasthānam (1.3)

"Then the seer is established in his own true nature."

Again, the message is clear. Make the manas/mind transparent, and immediately the Self will be revealed behind it. The manas/mind and its samskaras are a veil, masking the Self.

If we analyse the functioning of samskaras in terms of this simple model of subtle bodies, what do we find? Let us look again at the example of the fridge's noise that reminds you of Brünnhilde coming for lunch. The sound is first received through our physical ears. From the physical body, the perception is transmitted to the layer of energy, the etheric body, and reaches the layer of mental consciousness and emotions (astral body). At this stage, however, a short-circuit takes place. Instead of being felt from the Self, the sound is received by the manas/mind which creates an association, and a thought is generated – still in the astral body. Then another micro-samskara is triggered and another thought arises, always in the astral body.

Experientially, how does this manifest? You think without being aware that you think. The Self, layer of self-awareness, is left out of the process of thinking. By practising inner vigilance, this can easily be observed. There are times when you are aware, and if a thought arises in your mind you can just watch it and let go of it, without interrupting the flow of your awareness. At other times, you become caught by a train of thoughts. One thought arises, and another one after it, and you don't even realize that it is happening. It is not you who thinks, it is the thoughts that think themselves in your mind. Your awareness is lost, overpowered by the manas/mind. Only after a few minutes (or hours!) do you remember your purpose and restore the inner awareness.

The same process of bypassing the Self takes place even more obviously with emotions. For instance, a driver surprises you by honking when you least expect it. The sound is received by your ears (physical body), transmitted through the layer of energy (etheric body), and reaches your manas/mind. A fraction of a second later, you find yourself responding with an insult. The fact is that you were totally unaware of the samskara which was triggered and reacted. This clearly indicates that the layer of self-awareness was bypassed. The input went as far as the astral body, and a reactional output (the words of insult) mechanically followed. The highest of the four vehicles, that of self-awareness, was short-circuited.

Between the thoughts and emotions of the manas/mind and the self-awareness, the relationship can be described as 'eater/eaten'. You can either react or be aware, but the two are opposed. When you react your awareness is lost, as if eaten. It is no exaggeration to describe the manas/mind as the eater of the Self. Through the work of self-transformation, this relationship is slowly inverted. The layer of self-awareness matures into an unfathomable Self that can neutralise any wave of the manas/mind even before it arises. As one of the fundamental texts of Vedanta puts it, the Self becomes the 'eater', the 'devourer' of everything (*Brahma-Sutra* 1.2.9).

4.4 Feeling, Self and unity

In contrast to emotions, feelings are endowed with a sense of Self. As far as feelings are concerned, there are many degrees. Some feelings have just a hue of self-awareness, hardly more than a background. Others connect you with the deepest level and make your Self shine like a sun. However, the common thread to all feelings is that, unlike emotions, they do not conceal the Self but reveal it. Feelings establish an experiential link with the 'little flame', the eternal presence of the Self in the heart – whereas emotions take place in the surface personality, the facade.

This suggests that emotions keep you separated from the person or the circumstances that trigger them, for in an emotion, your Self is simply not present. It is kept away from the action. How could there be unity between your Self and the situation, when your Self is not there?

A feeling, on the other hand, creates a unity between you and the object or person that it relates to. Let us say that you are watching the myriads of stars in a night sky, and the beauty of the moment generates an inner wave; suddenly you are part of the universe. There is a strong and tangible sense of unity with the starry sky. That is a feeling. Just before, you were looking at the constellations, and they were nothing more than white dots on a dark background. Maybe you were learning to recognize their positions, or maybe you were caught in other thoughts, hardly aware of the stars. You were looking from the manas/mind. On one side, there was you on the ground, and on the other side, the white dots. Now, suddenly, a deeper part of yourself awakens with an intimate feeling of your unity with the cosmos. Your whole perception is transformed, as if you were in a different space. The universe suddenly makes sense to the soul. A feeling is arising.

Let us take another example, something that will happen to more and more therapists in the coming decades, and that might create a revolution in the art of diagnosis. A friend or a client comes to see you with a pain somewhere in his body. You feel just an intense compassion for him. You are in your heart, forgetting all your personal problems for a while, and being as open as you can. Then, without having to ask any questions, you suddenly realize that you are feeling where the pain is. It is not even that you know where the pain is, you *feel* it! You feel his body as if it were your own. There is a wave of unity between the two of you and as a practical result you have a flash of, not clairvoyance or clairaudience, but 'clairfeeling'. You feel what your friend feels as if you were in his body. For these experiences to take place, you need to be able to totally forget about your own difficulties and emotions for a moment, and be there only for the other, opening to him or her from your heart without any restriction.

A crucial point about 'clairfeeling' is that you feel the pain and emotions of the other person, but to you there is no suffering associated with them. The friend experiences the pain from his level of emotions (the manas/mind), but you receive it from your layer of feeling. You are not suffering with him, you are with him while he is suffering, which is quite different. It is a closeness, an opening from heart to heart, by which you hold the other one's intensity close to your Spirit. But there is nothing unpleasant or painful for you in this state.

One of the main purposes of the ISIS techniques of regression is to help you develop this ability to feel what others experience in their body and mind, from such a space of higher compassion. While playing the role of the connector, it will happen more and more that you feel a sensation or receive an image just before the client mentions it. These moments of 'shared perception' often go with a tangible sense that your Higher Self is present and participating in the process.

Essentially, feeling is a mode of knowledge through unity. It has to do with tuning into an object or a person and letting their qualities become alive inside your own Self. More than just resonating with the object, it is an experience of metaphysical unity. There are degrees in such experiences of course, but as your capacity to feel grows, this perception of unity becomes clearer and clearer.

The unity associated with feelings gives you the capacity to understand things and beings from inside. You stop looking at them from outside and being amazed at the differences between you and them. If, through feeling, you can 'become one' with what they are, be it only for a short moment, then you cannot remain a stranger to them. This perception, without which love can only be a facade, entails a deep metaphysical acceptance of situations and people. You may not agree with what a person says or does. You may work in a different direction and with opposite objectives. Still, feeling makes you experience a one-ness with that person. You do what you have to do, even if it does not serve that person's interests; but you participate in the cosmic plan, because your action is based on recognising that person's essential nature – not on denying it.

As you advance in the work, you start to experience an unexpectedly vast range of feelings and sensations, because you open to various modalities far beyond the usual limits of the mind. On the level of the manas/mind and its emotions, you can only understand what is similar to your own patterns to a certain extent. If something or somebody is too foreign to your own experience, then it becomes a complete mystery. The mind can't even get a sense of how it would feel to be like that. Feeling, on the other hand, is not bound by such rigid limitations and opens your inner universe to all sorts of new realisations.

4.5 The vast range of feelings

This last point is important, because it corrects a false idea that many people implicitly have about themselves. They tend to think that on the one hand there are emotions; and on the other, uncondi- tional love and compassion – as if these two were the only possible feelings. Of course, the idea of unconditional love is very nice, but try to imagine a life in which all spicy emotions would be replaced by unconditional love and nothing else. The tableau would be appall- ingly boring – an insipid paradise in which everybody would be locked into the same feeling.

In reality it is exactly the opposite. As you develop your capac- ity to feel, you become able to tune into all sorts of people and know what they experience inside yourself. Then the striking discovery is precisely that everybody seems more or less locked into a certain range of emotions which do not vary much from one person to the other. It gives the impression of barely a dozen musical notes end- lessly repeated by millions and millions of people who are impris- oned in their emotions as in a cage, and unable to open to anything else.

In contrast, feelings appear as a vast and fluid range of states and experiences. Being a mode of knowledge through identity, feel- ings allow you to resonate with various new frequencies beyond the usual limitations of the mind. This does not only apply to tuning into other people, but also everything around you – animals, plants and inanimate objects. This ability for feeling will result in a shower of gifts such as increased artistic sensitivity and creativity, greater toler- ance and understanding for others. Paradoxically, human beings ac- quire much more originality when they open to the sphere of the feelings, for they start to experience more varied and refined modalities of being.

4.6 The layer of feelings and the alchemy of the astral body

We have described how emotions pertain to the manas/mind, which corresponds to the layer of the astral body. Let us now envisage the layer in which the feelings take place.

Even though they have a direct connection with the Self, or Ego, feelings pertain to a different layer. To use the analogy of an electric light bulb, the bulb itself could be seen as the Self, while feelings are akin to the light radiating from it. Feelings pertain to a sphere in which the Self finds expression, cognizes the world and responds to it.[1]

In the system of Rudolf Steiner, the Spirit-Self is what corresponds to the layer of feelings. Unfortunately, following theosophical terminology, Steiner sometimes used the word manas synonymously with Spirit-Self. This is quite misleading, for in Sanskrit manas means precisely the opposite – the layer of reactional thinking and emotions.

To summarise, just as the astral body is the layer of emotions and thinking (reactional thinking), so the Spirit-Self, or *vijñāna-maya-kośa*, is made of feelings. The beginning of enlightenment consists of replacing the astral body with this new layer which, presently, is not very developed in most human beings.

---

[1] In the system of Vedanta, this layer of the feelings corresponds to *vijñāna-maya-kośa*. *Kośa* means sheath or envelope, *maya* means made of, and *vijñāna* is one of those Sanskrit words which should not be translated too hastily, for it does not really have any equivalent in modern European languages. Thus the usual translation of *vijñāna* as 'discernment', or 'discerning knowledge', is quite inappropriate and misleading. What is usually meant by discernment corresponds to a quality of the manas/mind, not to *vijñāna*. A more appropriate western equivalent for *vijñāna* would be the Greek word *gnosis*. *Gnosis* refers to a form of knowledge based on direct experience of spiritual realities, beyond the limitations of dogma and the screen of the rational mind. *Gnosis* has often been described as a 'knowledge of the heart', and corresponds to the knowledge through identity that we have described above. In the terminology used in this book, *gnosis* and feeling are one and the same thing.

From the point of view of inner alchemy, this means building up a new vehicle, a 'transformed astral body', seat of feelings. The term 'transformed astral body' is somehow misleading, for it gives the idea that the new layer will be made out of the old astral body after some process of transformation, which is not correct. The new layer is made out of the very substance of the Self (Ego), secreted from the Self the same way a spider secretes its web, according to an example often developed in the Hindu tradition. So, rather than transformed astral body, it would be more appropriate to use the term transubstantiated astral body.

A parallel can be drawn with the alchemists' quest for gold. In astrological and alchemical symbolism, gold stands for the Sun, which is none other than the Spirit, or Self, or Ego. Pursuing the same analogy, base metals can be related to the passions, emotions and reactions of the astral body. Turning base metals into gold corresponds to the transformation through which the astral body is replaced by the Spirit-Self, or transubstantiated astral body.

Because it is made of the gold of the Spirit, the transubstantiated astral body (layer of feelings), remains untouched by emotional fluctuations and can keep its integrity through the process of death. It can therefore properly be called a vehicle of immortality, or body of immortality. This is not yet physical immortality, for which a number of other layers would have to be transformed. Still, the transubstantiated astral body is a vehicle through which the transition of death can be made in full awareness, and the consciousness and experiences of this life can be kept and transferred into the following life without the astral disintegration that usually takes place with death.

The perspective of the Clairvision techniques is resolutely alchemical. A central purpose of ISIS is to help you discern between emotions and feelings, in order to start working at the transmutation of the astral body into the alchemical gold, the transubstantiated astral body.

Before dealing with this point and going one step further into the mechanisms of the mind, let us summarise the topic of emotions and feelings in the form of a table.

Emotions	Feelings
✦ anger, jealousy, passionate love...	✦ higher love, compassion, warmth of soul, enthusiasm, aesthetic feelings...
✦ are reactional	✦ are unconditional
✦ can quickly transform into their opposite	✦ are stable regardless of feedback
✦ come from the trigger of a samskara	✦ arise independently of samskaras
✦ generate more samskaras	✦ do not create any more samskaras
✦ are based on grasping	✦ are based on letting go
✦ overshadow the Higher Self and reinforce the tie with the astral body	✦ resonate with the Higher Self and reinforce the link with it
✦ favour and are favoured by lack of awareness	✦ enhance and are enhanced by awareness
✦ de-centre have a centrifugal direction (away from the Self)	✦ re-centre have a centripetal direction (toward the Self)
✦ cut you off from your environment	✦ establish a unity with the object
✦ cause a distorted perception of reality due to samskaric interference	✦ objectivity rediscovered in the deepest subjectivity
✦ make you live in 'your' world	✦ allow you to live in 'the' world

Let us also use a table to summarise the parallels with other systems.

	Emotions	Feelings
Clairvision language	astral body personal stage	transformed astral body transpersonal stage
Sanskrit	*mano-maya-kośa*, envelope made of manas	*vijñāna-maya-kośa*, envelope made of *buddhi*
Greek	*dianoia*, the discursive mind	*nous*, Greek equivalent of *budhhi*
Scholastic Latin	*ratio*	*intellectus*
Kabbalah	*nefesh* and *ruah*	*neshamah*
Rudolf Steiner	astral body	Spirit-Self

CHAPTER 5

SAMSKARAS AND MEDITATION

5.1 The monkey connection

Once upon a time there was a man in India who became very enthusiastic about finding his Self and decided to find a master and reach enlightenment. He inquired about all the gurus of the state, until he was told of one who was renowned as the wisest and most enlightened of his time. Off he went to the ashram of the holy man. As soon as he arrived, the guru asked him the traditional question,

"What have you come to seek here?"

The man was very straight. "Guruji, I have heard that you are a great sage. Will you give me enlightenment?"

The guru smiled. "Certainly, son, I will give you enlightenment."

The new disciple was transported with joy. "That's wonderful Guruji! Thank you, thank you very much. And what will I have to do to become enlightened?"

"Just go and sit under that tree and meditate."

"And what will I have to do to meditate?"

"Nothing, son. Just sit under the tree with your eyes closed. But whatever you do, do not think of monkeys. That's all. And you will reach enlightenment."

Our man was so delighted with the news of his imminent enlightenment that he forgot about his suitcase and went to sit under the tree straight away. And he began his meditation process.

However, ten seconds after he had sat in a beautiful lotus position and closed his eyes, a first monkey appeared to him in meditation. He immediately chased it away from his mind, but ten seconds later another monkey appeared inside; and another one; and another one... To his greatest embarrassment, after half an hour, the man had seen every possible Indian monkey. And then, relentlessly, his mind started sending him images of African monkeys. After another hour, and a few thousand more monkeys, the new disciple decided the case was hopeless and went back to the master.

"Guruji, you have to tell me more about the nature of the mind!"

After which the guru started to instruct him in the lore of samskaras.

5.2 Cogito ergo non sum, *I think therefore I am not*

Making the mind completely silent is not at all impossible, but it requires a shift into a different state of consciousness. As long as you remain in the usual layer of the manas/mind, trying to block the flow of thoughts is a notoriously hopeless enterprise. The more you attempt to fight it, the more the mind rebels and sends thoughts to your consciousness. If you have never experienced it for yourself, try to sit for a few minutes with the firm resolve not to think, like the beginner-disciple of our story. You will soon be convinced that trying to stop the mind while operating from the mind is a sheer waste of time.

As we saw previously, these constant mental fluctuations are called *vṛttis* in Sanskrit. The root *vṛt* means to turn, and the suffix '-ti' is used to generate action nouns. Therefore *vṛtti* means the action of turning, the fact of turning. The word is quite appropriate, for each of these little fluctuations, or *vṛttis*, tends to turn your mind in a slightly different direction. One *vṛtti* comes, and another one, and another one... and if you are not vigilant, a few minutes later you find yourself in a completely different state of mind.

As long as your consciousness is taking place in the manas/mind, the reason why it is impossible to stop the *vṛttis* is quite simple – the manas/mind is *made* of *vṛttis*. This layer of emotions and thinking acts as a veil hiding the Self, as pointed out in the first verses of Patañjali's *Yoga-Sūtras*: "Make the veil of the *vṛttis* drop, and immediately your real nature is revealed." As long as the manas/mind perpetuates its endless dance, you remain assimilated with the *vṛttis*. This means that your consciousness has been infested by the *vṛttis* for so long that you can't even imagine that you may

53

exist beyond them. You come to believe that thinking means being, whereas it is precisely when you are in the manas/mind that you are disconnected from the Self.

A man who came to be regarded as one of the fathers of rational thinking, French seventeenth-century philosopher René Descartes, had impressed generations of philosophers with the statement *cogito ergo sum*, "I think therefore I am".

Three and a half centuries later, the time has come to give ourselves a fresh start with the opposite claim, *cogito ergo non sum*, "I think, therefore I am not". Sorry Monsieur Descartes, but it is precisely when we stop thinking that we start to be. If there is a layer that can be said to *be*, it is that of the Self. As long as we are caught in the mental fluctuations of the manas/mind, we are disconnected from the Self.

Once more, this does not mean that the purpose of the work is to eradicate any form of thinking, but rather to replace the mechanical and unceasing thoughts of the reacting mind by the luminous thinking of the transformed (or transubstantiated) astral body. These two forms of thinking are so radically different that it is quite misleading to use the same word for both, just as 'emotion' cannot be used for both the love of the cat and that of Christ. One of the characteristics of the thinking of the transformed astral body is that it can be switched off at will. Unlike the thinking of the manas/mind, it does not happen mechanically and involuntarily, but is a fully conscious act of will.

5.3 Neutralising major samskaras to pacify the mind

The *vṛttis* are of major interest for our study of the mechanisms of the mind in relation to regression, for they are a direct indicator of the presence and dynamism of the samskaras. We have described the manas/mind as being made of reactions: reactional thoughts and reactional emotions. The manas/mind is full of waves of reactions, and the *vṛttis* are these waves. Just as on the ocean there are big waves and ripples, so in the manas/mind there are major reactions caused by big samskaras, and endless ripples caused by myriads of micro-samskaras.

A key realisation is that **the astral body is *made* of samskaras**. Its very nature is grasping and reacting, and its substance is like a sea of samskaras, some big, some small, some more linked to emotions, others more to thoughts. Even though the astral body lacks unity and consists of a bunch of dissimilar and ill-matched patches, all its parts are closely interrelated. For example, suppose you are affected by a strong emotion after quarrelling with someone in your family. If, just after the episode, you sit and try to meditate, your mind will be much more agitated than usual by thoughts. Many of these thoughts won't have any connection with the present situation. They will be regular *vrttis*, but quicker and more intense than usual.

What is happening? The emotion is stirring the whole layer of the reacting mind, resulting in an increased activity of the *vrttis*. The sea is agitated in depth, therefore its whole surface is covered with waves. Another way of putting it is that an intense emotional charge has been triggered, and this is feeding all the other samskaras. It is as if the tension had been increased in the reacting mind, making a higher voltage and intensity available to all the other samskaras. The result is an increased activity of *vrttis* of various kinds.

This observation is significant; it provides a clue for reaching mental silence during meditation. Clearly, we want to get rid of the *vrttis* in order to discover the Self that is hidden behind them. We have found the source of our perpetual thinking to be the countless micro-samskaras of which the very substance of the mind is woven. But if we had to eradicate each and every micro-samskara before we could reach mental peace, the task would be endless, simply because one cannot empty an ocean with a teaspoon. The situation is quite different. It is not the limitless number of micro-samskaras that makes the mind uncontrollable, but the fact that these micro-samskaras are fed by the emotional charges of a limited number of big ones.

If you cannot make your mind quiet, it is not so much because it is made of micro-samskaras. By themselves, these micro-samskaras would not be strong enough to keep your mind frantic. They would certainly create waves in your consciousness, but you could just watch them and let them fade, without losing your thread of self-awareness. If you have no mental peace it is because a few storms are permanently going on in your reacting mind, due to the emotional charges associated with a limited number of huge sam-skaras. You may not see them, not being aware of their presence because they have been operating in your mind almost constantly ever since you can remember. However, it is their energy that feeds all the other micro-samskaras and makes the reacting mind uncontrollable due to excessive voltage. More than ninety-nine per cent of your mental entropy is due to less than one per cent of your samskaras and the vicious intensity they spread.

This suggests that it is not necessarily by meditating forever that you will reach a state of meditation proper – beyond the manas/mind – but by looking at this one per cent of noxiously intense samskaras and neutralising them. If you have been meditating for a number of years without any decisive result, you should ponder upon this point, for it might save you another twenty years of meditation that leads nowhere.

5.4 To what extent can meditation neutralise samskaras?

The question that logically follows is: isn't it enough to meditate in order to neutralise samskaras, whether they are big or small? This is a key question, for it allows you to understand the major role that regression can play in a spiritual path.

In theory, yes, a proper system of meditation is supposed to allow you to clear the totality of your mind. Some signs indicate that a release is taking place; for instance when you start twitching, or when certain emotional or mental activities are going on while you meditate, it may mean that you are releasing some samskaras. Of course, one should not be too optimistic about this last point. It is unfortunately not enough to have one's mind churned by thoughts to be sure that one is releasing samskaras. Yet, overall, and even without twitching or special mental activity, the general direction of meditation is to release tension, grasping and samskaras. Each time you sit and meditate some samskaras are freed and neutralised.

In practice, however, the situation is far from being that simple, due to several important factors. First, you usually meditate only once or twice a day. Even if you meditate two hours twice a day, which is already quite respectable, it is quite easy for your mind to hide the major samskaras during the meditation time and let them loose during the remaining twenty hours. This is a gentle warning to people who believe that it is enough to meditate twice a day for a great spiritual transformation to ensue, without having to maintain any particular awareness the rest of the time. The manas/mind is outrageously clever, and if you offer it any opportunity to trick you, you may be sure it will grasp it. Nothing is easier for it than to make a deal with you such as "I will give you a beautiful meditative peace twice a day, and you will let me go on playing my games the rest of the time". You cannot find a better foundation than this for the type of spiritual practice that goes on for twenty years without any decisive opening. There may be improvements in your memory, your quality of sleep and your blood pressure – but the same results could be achieved with a few Hatha-Yoga postures and a bit of relaxation. The great spiritual shifts never happen, simply because the great samskaras remain untouched by the process.

The situation becomes quite different if, in addition to your daily meditation, you apply yourself to remaining aware and watching your mind react from morning to night. Then it is much more difficult for the reacting mind to manipulate you with samskaras without you realising what is going on.

Even if you could remain permanently aware, or if you could meditate from morning to night, the fact is that major samskaras excel at encapsulating and protecting themselves. If an experience has been traumatic enough to leave a major samskaric imprint, the reacting mind will use any trick possible to bury the imprint and make it inaccessible to your consciousness. The nature of the manas/mind is such that it will do anything to avoid facing its own contradictions. For this, it uses a whole range of mechanisms of protection. The paradox is that in many cases, the protective mechanisms themselves end up being significantly more painful, costing more energy than it would take to find the source of the problem and 'digest it' from the level of self-awareness. So each time you come close to seeing the samskara, the mind diverts your awareness. If nothing drastic is done, this situation can be perpetuated during years and years of meditation. You certainly release samskaras during meditation, but they are usually minor ones. The major ones remain unseen.

Fundamentally, meditation techniques aim at developing self-awareness and, in certain cases, building up subtle bodies. However, they are not specifically designed to put you in touch with samskaras. To illustrate this point, I will use the example of a boat, and the force that is needed to get it to move. You can spend one hour every day rowing; if the boat is anchored, twenty years later you will still be in the same place. Meditation is a process that makes you move towards the light in a general way, without specifically concentrating on the ties that keep you back. The example of the boat shows that the solution is not only to row, but to get rid of the anchor.

Of course, you could think of another solution. You could pull the boat with so much force that the tie of the anchor would break. That would mean increasing the power of your meditation to such an extent that even the major samskaras couldn't resist, and would explode in your consciousness. The problem is that to reach such an intensity of meditation, you would first have to get rid of your major samskaras, for they are the main limiting factor. It is obviously a vicious circle.

Even if you could become a full-time ascetic and do nothing other than meditate from morning to night for months – which would possibly allow you to reach the required intensity – there would still be something conceptually wrong with exhausting your energy trying to pull the boat while anchored. Why not raise the anchor first, and then go wherever you want? As soon as a handful of highly emotionally charged samskaras have been neutralised, your mind suddenly becomes incomparably quieter, allowing a much greater depth of meditation.

Another point that should be clearly understood is that the influence of samskaras has become much stronger than it used to be a few generations ago. In terms of our example, it is not only one rope but dozens, if not hundreds of ropes that keep us anchored close to the shore, and the ties have become more solid. In particular, the meditation techniques imported by most eastern masters were designed for disciples whose emotions were certainly not as harsh and violent as ours are now in the West. A few centuries ago in India, an ascetic could probably engage in spiritual practice without having to worry about whether his emotional blockages were going to suppress the intensity of his meditation. However, times have changed. The general level of people's neurosis has increased to such proportions that it has become unrealistic to deny the psychological dimension in a spiritual path, and to try to reach enlightenment without working systematically on eradicating wrong emotional patterns.

I am certainly not suggesting that regression should replace meditation, but that by combining the two, immense time and effort can be saved in a spiritual path. The present condition of the human astral body is such that by not dealing specifically with samskaras, you place yourself in the position of trying to row the boat without raising the anchor.

5.5 The manifestation of samskaras in meditation

There are many ways in which samskaras manifest while you are meditating, since all the reactions of the manas/mind can be sourced to samskaras. Apart from thoughts in meditation, let me draw your attention to two particular mechanisms.

One common way in which samskaras manifest during meditation is through pain in various body parts. If you have applied yourself to meditating for long periods, say five hours or more per day for at least a week, you will have noticed that numerous pains arise, sometimes in the most unsuspected areas of the body. Parts of your body in which you normally never feel any discomfort suddenly become terribly painful.

These meditation pains have a few unusual characteristics. Firstly, they appear only during meditation, and usually cease as soon as you get out of the meditative state. Secondly, they are often quite illogical. For example, you may suddenly feel a pain in your left shoulder while sitting in a position which should have no direct effect on this part of your body. Thirdly, these pains are extremely stubborn. When following a prolonged course of meditation, you may feel the same pain in the same place every single day, every single hour you meditate, for days and days without any relief. Fourthly, the main feature of these pains is that they increase with the energy of your meditation. The deeper your meditation and the more you connect with the energy, the worse the pain gets. As soon as you stop meditating, the pain stops.

These meditation pains come straight from samskaras. They indicate that your meditation has been deep enough to contact one of your major samskaras, and that a 'fight' is going on between the samskara and the light. To return to our example, you are the boat; the light of higher consciousness is pulling you, but the samskara is obstinately resisting, like the anchor pulling you back. In many cases this can last for years. Each time you build up the meditation energy, the pain reappears. Each time you release the pressure of the energy – for instance if you stop meditating or if you fidget instead of remaining connected – the pain diminishes or stops. The pattern becomes especially drastic when you endeavour to meditate from morning to night for a few weeks or months; the intensity of the pain can take proportions that are simply unreasonable. Unless you undergo such an experience, you just cannot know how much pain it is possible to feel in your body. At this stage, you can usually realise that the pain is not only physical, but accompanied by an emotional pressure. But in most cases you lack the dynamic energy to release it, simply because your meditation has been designed to pull you towards the light, not to deal with samskaras.

At the beginning of an ISIS session, before entering the regression state, it is quite common for clients to experience pains of this kind in various parts of the body. The technical term used for these painful areas is 'spot'. The spots are direct manifestations of samskaras – the mechanisms behind them are identical to those behind the pains that arise in deep meditation.

The energy of ISIS, however, operates differently from that of meditation. It does not act as a general uplifter, but is endowed with a special dynamism designed to reveal the samskaras and neutralise their power. In other words, it is an energy that does not work at rowing the boat, but one that specialises in dealing with anchors. Thus the experience will be completely different; instead of feeling the pain and nothing else, the pain will quickly turn into an emotion. For instance, you will feel an intense grief, or anger. You will reconnect with the emotional charge attached to the samskara.

At this stage, a common experience is that the pain completely disappears, which can be quite disconcerting for beginners. How could they feel such intense pain a few seconds ago, and have the pain vanish as soon as they become aware of the emotion? The disappearance of the pain indicates that the layer encapsulating the samskara has been removed. You have reconnected with the emotion, and all the circumstances related to the traumatic episode start coming back to your consciousness. Consequently, there is no longer any need for protection mechanisms. The conditions are gathered for a release of the emotional charge associated with the samskara.

In this way meditation and regression can work together. Through meditation, spots (latent samskaras) are revealed, and through regression they are released. These releases allow a deeper quality of meditation, in which deeper samskaras can be contacted, and so on.

Of course, you do not need to meditate to get in touch with samskaras. Just go through normal life, observe your reactions, and the circumstances of life will bring about many emotions that relate to your samskaras. However it should be clear that by practising meditation regularly, you get in touch with much deeper issues. This is why people who have done a lot of meditation can have such quick results when they undergo a regression process. Their meditation not only allows them to deal with a number of minor issues, but also to get in touch with the real monsters of the depths, the 'capital samskaras'. They lack the specialised dynamic energy to deal with them, but they have made contact with them, which is a crucial step in the process.

Conversely, people who have gone through many regressions will be surprised to discover completely new samskaras and unsuspected core issues after experiencing in-depth meditation. Just as regression can be a powerful complement to meditation, so meditation will greatly enhance the depth of regression.

5.6 Waves

Let us now examine another mechanism through which samskaras manifest during meditation. The experience we are going to describe is of critical importance. Depending on how you handle it, it can lead to great progress, or to even greater mistakes. The mechanism has to do with huge emotional waves that suddenly sweep your consciousness when you reach a certain depth in meditation.

The kind of meditative states we are now discussing cannot be achieved just by meditating for a few hours a day, whatever your technique may be. For these waves to take place, you usually need a total withdrawal from activity, doing nothing but meditation for at least a few weeks. The experience requires total isolation, or at least that you do not speak during that period. There should be nothing to distract your mind, no activities taking place around you, no telephone, no mail – just meditating, eating, and sleeping. In some initiation practices, this is carried out in an underground crypt, in absolute darkness; the surrounding rock provides isolation from all the vibrations of the world.

The principles behind this practice are clear; to a large extent, you are the product of your environment. A vast part of your emotions and thought patterns come from what your parents, friends and partners have imprinted in you, as well as from all the sensory impressions collected since you were born. One wonders, therefore, what exists beyond this accumulation of input and imprints. What exactly is left of you, if these are taken away? What, inside you, is eternal and not merely the product of your environment?

Of course, such an intensive period of meditation should not be attempted without sufficient preparation. It is only once you have gone through sustained work on yourself and have achieved a fair degree of emotional stability that such long periods of full-time meditation may be attempted. Furthermore, even though we are reaching an age of self-initiation, I would still recommend that you seek the advice and protection of a competent guide before dealing with explosive practices of this kind.

What happens after a few weeks of full-time meditation and isolation? You discover some completely new modalities of yourself. From time to time, openings of consciousness take place, and you realise that up till then you had always existed within a certain frame, without ever crossing its limits. The atmosphere, flavour and stereotyped routines in your head had always been the same; but you had not even noticed them, simply because you were lacking references. Having never experienced anything else, you believed that it was all one could be. Then you suddenly realise that one can be completely different. To take an analogy dear to Hindu masters, until then you had only seen the world with green-coloured glasses. Now you discover that you can also see it through yellow glasses, blue glasses, or even without glasses at all!

Along with these openings, another experience is likely to take place – unexpected, sudden, and utterly violent waves of emotions or desires. For instance, you are suddenly taken by an irresistible desire to go back into the world and study Taoism. Within one minute, it becomes the most important thing in your life – the one thing you want and which seems to hold the key to complete fulfilment. It is as if you had reached an absolute inner certitude as to which direction to follow. While you are supposedly meditating, your mind starts fixing up all the details frantically: what books to read first, how to enrol in the next course in Chinese at university, where to buy Chinese-looking clothes, and how to find a Taoist master.

Then, a few hours later, something very surprising takes place; another wave emerges, completely different from the first one. You suddenly feel the irresistible need to take the first plane to New York, join a friend you have not seen for fifteen years, and get married. Taoism has completely disappeared from your mind, and the former certitude has been replaced by a new one: the only thing that will ever fulfil your life is to go and marry that person – who had never really been a close friend before, and whom you have not seen for more than fifteen years. Your meditation changes. The mind gets hyperactive arranging all the details of the trip: the travel agent from whom you will get the plane ticket, what you will wear at the wedding, what names to give the children, and so on.

If you can resist these emotional onslaughts and remain in your meditation retreat instead of taking the first plane to New York, what happens? A few hours, or maybe one day later, another tidal wave sweeps your consciousness and you want to start a publishing company, or take up dramatic art, or become a Methodist minister or a politician.

The most striking thing about these waves is their intensity. They seem to be coming out of nowhere, and when you least expect them. Their violence pushes you to the limit of what you can bear. You really have to tap from your deepest resources to stay meditating instead of being carried away by them. Most people tend to believe they have received an unmistakable sign of destiny when they are struck by such a wave. They believe that they have found their true purpose in life.

It could take a whole life to fulfil any of these desires. That is one of the reasons why you have to be fully prepared before undergoing this type of long and intensive meditation practice. If you yield to the first wave and end up in Shanghai, which can happen awfully quickly under such circumstances, nothing good is likely to result. The decision to fly to China was not taken from a space of free will, but dictated by the pressure of a samskara. Sooner or later, another samskara will take you in another direction. If you let your life be ruled by the kaleidoscope of the manas/mind, the overall result can only be chaos. Even if you happened to be successful in China, that would be a 'samskara-success'. Your spiritual thread would be lost, and it might take twenty years before you found it again.

If, on the other hand, you can resist the first waves and remain firm in your meditation, the following ones will have less power over you. You will be able to compare them to the first ones and convince yourself that something unusual is going on. Yet, however well prepared you may be, you will probably be taken aback by the cataclysmic intensity of the urges. These are the types of desires that people normally feel only once every twenty years, and which can make them change everything. Yet, in deep meditation a new wave can hit you every day, or even every few hours. Having had to withstand a dozen of them in a week, you *know* that they are the product of samskaras, and therefore fundamentally fake. Still it takes all of your determination and God's help not to yield to the thirteenth. Finally, after a time that varies greatly with each individual, the waves stop, and you discover you have become a completely different person.

The way these waves grasp you and make you frantic for a short while, before disappearing in an anticlimax and giving way to another one, leaves little doubt as to their real nature and source – these waves come from your deepest and most intense samskaras. Most people do not make much contact with these capital samskaras during their entire life. The pressure of your meditation makes the samskaras explode in your consciousness one after the other. In terms of our example, the force pulling the boat has become so intense that no tie can resist it. What most human beings can't achieve in several lives is completed in a few weeks.

Once the tidal waves have passed, what follows is the experience of being 'reborn'. So many emotional charges have been released that your mind has become totally different, as if tonnes and tonnes had been lifted off your head. You hardly recognise yourself. Your life has become incredibly simple.

5.7 No major decisions during a meditation intensive

To be able to deal with such waves without being carried away, you need to have already done significant work on your samskaras. The more you have observed your samskaras, watched your own reactions in daily situations and looked for the sources of your conditioned behaviour, the less chance you have of being distracted by the Sirens[1] when the 'hour of God' comes. In this respect the regression work is one of the best possible preparations for withstanding the spiritual intensity of the moments of great awakening, and avoiding the first samskara booby-trap.

Given the nature of these samskaric waves, it is wise not to make any important life decisions whenever undergoing a meditation retreat or an intense regression process. Even though on a much lower scale, similar waves of desire may be triggered. If you were to yield to a wave and make major decisions at that time, you might well regret it bitterly later on. Once more, such decisions would not be based on free will and on the real aspirations of your Self, but on the tyranny of samskaras. Wisdom commends finishing the meditation retreat or the regression intensive first, and then taking a few weeks before making any major decision.

5.8 A note about knees

The knees are an exception to the pattern of deep pains that occur in meditation due to the emergence of samskaras.

If a spot in the shoulder, the back, or any other body part but the knees becomes sore under the pressure of deep meditation, the best attitude is to remain motionless and watch the spot. Just remain aware of it; by fidgeting you would be diminishing the pressure of the energy and avoiding the samskara. Simply watch the spot, and let it ripen through your stillness and awareness. If it does not disappear, regress it! In any case, you will not damage your body by remaining still and putting up with the intensity created by a samskara.

If, however, you are sitting in lotus, semi-lotus, or any other crossed-legged position, the situation is quite different as far as your

---

[1] This experience presents obvious similarities with Odysseus' encounter with the Sirens, when his crew had to tie him to the boat to stop him jumping into the water in response to the Sirens' enticing call.

knees are concerned. Have a good look at somebody taking the lotus position. What happens when they place their heel close to the groin? It is not the knee joint that rotates, it is the hip. Contrary to what one might think, it is from the flexibility of the hips that the lotus position is achieved – not the knees. The articulation of the knee is made of tiny ligaments which can't be stretched much without damage.

If after meditating for some time you start feeling pain in the knees, it is because the hip has contracted. The hip has rotated inwards, which results in more tension on the knee ligaments. These little ligaments are fragile, and it is unwise to try to pull them beyond their limits. If you damage one of them, it could take months before you are able to sit cross-legged again.

The conclusion is that a pain in the knees should always be respected. If your knees start hurting while meditating cross-legged, change position. Sit on a chair if needed. Stoically putting up with the pain in order to remain motionless is likely to cause more harm than good.

CHAPTER 6

SAMSKARAS AND PHYSICAL DISORDERS

6.1 An example of physical pain created by samskaras

Case study – Lenka was a forty-six-year-old business woman, who came to consult me after years of heavy depression. Among her somatic complaints were terrible headaches in the forehead that nothing seemed to alleviate, and bad colic pains. Before coming to me and trying the ISIS technique of regression, Lenka had sought the help of a number of therapists unsuccessfully.

Soon after the beginning of the first session, an excruciatingly painful spot was located in her left ribcage area. As Lenka connected more deeply with the energy, the spot suddenly triggered her usual head-ache and intestinal pain with extreme violence. It must be stressed that at no time in the session did I touch Lenka's head or abdomen; and on no occasion prior to this ISIS session had Lenka experienced any discomfort in the area of her left ribcage.

After a moment of agonising pain, working on the spot, the quality of vibration in the room suddenly changed, and Lenka started reexperiencing an episode with particularly vivid intensity.

What are you feeling?[1] –I'm cold, I'm so cold. [Lenka is shivering under a pile of blankets.] Something very big has fallen on me and buried me. It's a rock. My head hurts. And there is a fire. Lots of people are being killed... scenes of devastation. There has been an

---

[1] As before, the questions at the beginning of the paragraphs are asked by the connector. The answers are those made by the client.

earthquake and now there is a fire, but I'm buried underneath the rock so I'm not being burnt.

Now there is water coming. The fire is finished. I can't move because I'm buried under the stone, and there is water coming over me. Oh! It's terribly cold [Lenka is shivering more than ever.] It's absolutely freezing, freezing cold. [Screaming:] The baby! The baby is dying! It's me under the rock, but I'm pregnant with a baby. Oh! Pain... It's like feeling all my usual stomach pains at the same time.

Do you mean they are the same as your intestinal pains? –Same. The baby is dying! [Flood of tears.] The baby is coming out and there is no one to help. Oh! I wish I was dead. And it hurts, it hurts to deliver the baby. [Sobbing:] It's dead. I know the baby is dead. Oh! I've got the splitting headache again. [Screaming:] It hurts! It hurts! My head is cracked open, totally cracked open. It hurts! It's horrible! My brains are coming out! It's here! [Indicating the place in her forehead where she usually gets headaches:] My head is split open here. The rock... the rock has smashed my head. I wish I was dead. It feels like I should be dead, but for some reason I'm not. Oh God! It hurts so much!

After the session, Lenka told me how she had always been terrified of having a child, which suddenly started to make sense after reexperiencing this episode. She had been pregnant five times. Two of the pregnancies were aborted, while the other three ended up in miscarriage.

The results of this regression were spectacular. Within a few days both the headaches and the intestinal pains dropped by more than half. After a few weeks and a few more sessions, the headaches had almost completely disappeared. The depression started improving and Lenka got rid of all her pain-killers, tranquillisers and sleeping tablets.

6.2 Samskaras do not only manifest in the mind

In this chapter, we will see how some samskaras not only manifest through emotions and mental reactions, but also through disorders in the physical body.

In the last chapter we saw that in deep meditation, samskaras often create physical pain in various parts of the body, and that in ISIS, similar painful spots are experienced. But in ISIS, the situation is different. Instead of feeling the pain without ever realising what is behind it, a dynamic energy is activated which reveals the samskara behind the spot. In most cases, the pain stops as soon as the client connects with the emotion and the circumstances related to the samskara. This reconnection allows the client to neutralise the samskara by releasing its emotional charge.

These experiences are of great interest, for they allow clients to perceive for themselves how much samskaras can 'grasp' the physical body. The intensity of the physical manifestations during some regressions is such that clients can't have much doubt as to the interconnection between samskaras and the physical body. In the above example, Lenka simply could not believe that just by putting energy on a point in her chest, I could cause her headaches and stomach aches to be reproduced exactly. It was a clear demonstration that something other than just physical factors was causing her problems.

The concept of psychosomatic ailments, meaning the possibility of mental complexes creating physical disorders, is not new. The input regression provides in psychosomatic explorations is to offer a direct way of finding the real source of the disorder, often far beyond early childhood traumas. Consequently it allows profound releases and healing. The essence of regression is to go back to sources. As we will see, a cure can never really be regarded as complete as long as the source of the ailment has not been dealt with, no matter what therapy is implemented.

Before tackling the difficult question of determining what proportion of diseases may be due to samskaras, let us first examine the mechanisms by which a samskara creates a physical disorder. If we look at the pattern emerging from Lenka's regression, we see that it is quite similar to that of the samskara-related emotions we have already studied. Samskaras, by nature, tend to repeat the same 'message' endlessly. Their nature is akin to conditioning. If you have been abandoned and if you nearly died from it, the samskara tends to place you in situations where the same rejection drama is replayed again and again. If you have felt excessively alienated in a past life because you were crippled, your samskaras will make you feel alienated here and now, without any present logical reason for it. Many samskaric blockages act like prerecorded roles. As long as they are not eliminated, you remain caught in an endless replay of these roles.

If we analyse Lenka's case study, we can see that it follows exactly the same pattern. When practising regression, I have often observed that the loss of a child, especially around the time of delivery, leaves some of the deepest possible samskaras. Such a samskara manifested in Lenka's life in her fear of having children. Also the very dark emotional time when trapped under the rock resulted in a heavy depression that nothing seemed to alleviate until she underwent the regression process.

However, the initial traumatic episode not only consisted of emotional distress; it was accompanied by terrible physical pain. Her skull was broken open by the rock, and she endured the labour pain in the most horrid conditions. In this present life, when these samskaras were reactivated, Lenka's depression started. It was not only the emotional pain that was brought to the surface, but also physical disorders. Lenka started replaying her head trauma with headaches, and her labour pain with intestinal colic. The scheme is identical to that described for emotional patterns, but with an added physical dimension. A suffering of the past superimposes itself upon the present. Even though Lenka could not perceive it as long as she had not undergone an ISIS process, her physical disorders were none other than a replay of past circumstances.

From a medical point of view, it is essential to understand that the origin of Lenka's illness had little, if anything, to do with her intestines. We remain much closer to the truth if we call Lenka's trouble a 'tummy ache', not an intestinal disorder. It happened that in her case, twisting the chemistry of the bowels was the most direct way for the samskara to reproduce the labour pain. But the samskara could also have expressed itself by creating the same pain in another organ, for instance by creating a disorder in the gynaecological sphere, anything from premenstrual tension to endometriosis, or even cancer. This is typically a situation where a medical practitioner's rigid attitude which focuses on one single organ, be it intestine, uterus or whatever, completely misses the point and proves unable to bring about any lasting improvement.

6.3 Do accidents happen by accident?

In the case we have just examined, we see a client feeling almost exactly the same pain as in the episode that originated the samskara, but expressing it through a different organ and in different life circumstances. However, in some cases the parallel between the circumstances related to the samskara and those of the physical ailment in this life is even more obvious. In particular, the significance of many accidents is perceived quite differently after undergoing a regression process. Here is a short example, one of many similar ones I have encountered in my practice.

Case study – Lucie, aged forty-four, had suffered from an uncomfortable feeling in her left groin as far back as she could remember. It was a dull sensation, half-way between a pain and a tightness. No medical practitioner could ever find anything pathologically wrong with her, even though she sensed that there was something wrong. The following regression occurred while working on the left groin.

How does your body feel, big or small? –I feel very big; and very strong. A BIG man. He's totally enraged. It's in the middle of a battle, like in medieval times. There are people and bodies everywhere. He's fighting with something very heavy, a kind of mace, or maybe a sword. It's extremely heavy. He is completely furious. He's roaring and moving like a madman. He feels nothing can stop him, he's gonna kill them all!
[Then the client suddenly screams, as if in pain.] Ah! Something has hit him in the groin. The pain is terrible. He falls on his knees.
I can see him lying on his back. He can't move. There is something stuck inside his groin, like a piece of metal. It could be an arrow.
What's happening around him? –It feels far away. The battle is going on, but I hear it as if from a distance. I'm lying on my back, immobilised with that thing in my groin.[1] Now the battle is finished. I can see bodies everywhere. It's night. He is blocked, he can't go on.

---

[1] Notice how clients tend to alternate between the first and third person when describing themselves in a past-life episode.

He's half in, half out of his body, as if nailed to it by the arrow in his groin.

Does he stay there for a long time? –It feels like a long time. He knows he is dead and it does not feel right to remain there. His body is starting to rot. But he can't move away. The groin is keeping him back.

Coincidentally, Lucie had had an accident when she was in her thirties (about fifteen years after she had begun to feel the dull ache in the groin, so that the accident could not be held responsible for the discomfort in this area). She was hit by a car in her left hip, and suffered multiple fractures. It is not unreasonable to want to make a link between this trauma and the wound of the medieval warrior. Lucie herself made the connection as soon as this ISIS session was finished, "The pain in his groin felt exactly like mine when I had my accident".

Ever since I started practising regression, I have been struck by the number of occasions where accidents coincided with a similar trauma discovered by the client while reexperiencing a past-life episode. Knowing that it takes years to build up the field for cancer to develop in your body, it is not difficult to conceive how the manas/mind may play its part. But in a car accident, when someone's hip is broken in a fraction of a second, it is not so easy to conceive that the mind may be involved! Yet, whatever mechanism of synchronicity may be involved, dozens of similar examples have suggested that it is not by chance that some people break their left arm rather than their right leg, or their nose rather than their sacrum. On the contrary, many accidents seem to take place as if the trauma was prerecorded, and as if the person was unconsciously – but quite precisely – attracting the blow. In these cases, as long as the samskara is not neutralised it keeps on attracting trouble, just as a lamp attracts moths at night.

6.4 Different pains, same meridian

In this section we will look at how different physical disorders may appear from life to life along the line of the same acupuncture meridian.

Case study – Sophia is forty-one and suffers from bad sciatic pain in the right leg (*zu-shao-yang* meridian). The surgeons gave her a grim warning – unless operated on, she might end up in a wheelchair. However, she refused to undergo any form of surgery, and decided to cure herself by other means. Here is a passage from a key regression that changed the course of her illness.

What are you feeling now? –I'm feeling cold, very cold. [Even though it is a hot summer day in Sydney, Sophia is shivering with cold and asking for more blankets.] I was in the water, but now I have landed on the shore. There's nobody there. I'm all alone. I'm scared, and cold. It's a huge place. The beach seems to go on forever. I can see the sky.

Can you hear any sound? –Yes, the waves.

Any pain? –No, but numbness. I can't walk. I'm sitting with my legs stretched out but I can't get up. My right leg feels completely numb. I feel agitated. First I thought it was fear, but now it's more like feeling helpless. I don't know what to do! I can't stay there, it's leading me nowhere. But at the same time I can't move either, because of my leg. I'd like to be with the others, in the ship. I can't remember exactly what happened, how I got there. It's a sailor; and he is pretty stuck. He just can't move his right leg.

Is the feeling in the leg similar to what you feel now [in this twentieth-century Australian life]? –Yes. The numbness on the beach is exactly in the same area I feel the sciatic pain now [*zu-shao-yang* meridian].

Is it identical? –It is not the same pain, but the feeling behind both is exactly the same.

When you get the sciatic pain, do you also get any similar feelings to those of the man on the beach? –Yes, desperation. Because my pain never seems to go away. He felt desperate too because he had no way of escaping from that place. The feeling is the same.

When you feel the despair in this [present] life, is it yours or his? –It feels more like his. Actually, it is completely his.

From this example we see that the current violent pain of the client was not part of the original episode. All the sailor was feeling was numbness in the leg. Yet the location of Sophia's pain has remained the same (the line of the *zu-shao-yang* meridian on the external side of the thigh and the leg). So has the accompanying emotion, that is, the helpless despair.

Even though the client did not present the same symptoms as those of the stranded sailor, she had the feeling of a common 'flavour' linking the two. This is quite characteristic of physical pains which persist from one life to another. In similar cases, clients often make comments such as, "It's not the same pain, but the feeling behind it is the same" or "It's the same vibration." Such occurrences in regression are an extremely favourable sign; they indicate a great chance of improvement. They show that the client has contacted a samskara underlying the physical trouble. It is therefore likely that an improvement will take place once the samskara is released.

After this regression, the sciatic pain started to decrease significantly, but not totally. Some more episodes related to the same samskara were still to be discovered before a final healing could be achieved. Here is one of the regressions that followed.

At the beginning of the regression, Sophia seems to be going through a lot of pain. She is jerking and jumping as if struggling against invisible enemies.

What's happening now? –I can see people sitting around a fire. Somebody has taken a burning stick. He uses it to burn me there. [Sophia indicates a spot on the side of her right foot.] I'm sitting, and they are holding me. It is the same helpless feeling. I'm trying to defend myself, and then I stop fighting. [Sophia becomes still again.] Why? –I know they are not doing it to hurt me. I know I have to go through it. So I try to remain quiet. It looks like a cigar... now I don't feel the pain anymore. The cigar is still there but the pain has become much less. They did it as a treatment because I was wounded. The man with the cigar was some kind of doctor.

Is there any similarity between this pain and your sciatic pain? –Oh, yes, very much the same! But then it was in the foot, not in the leg. [In this present life,] I never feel pain in my foot.

What do these people look like? –Not big. Short dark hair. They are living in the desert. There are some women with them. They laugh at me gently and they give me something to drink. They say I have been very lucky they found me and treated me. It was an accident. I have been hit in the hip by something. A camel. I got kicked by a camel, and I was lying in the desert, completely helpless, unable to move. It is always the same feeling – I can't move, as if I was going to die there. It's sheer despair.

In this regression there was a significant element; the spot indicated by the client on her foot was the acupuncture point *zu-shao-yang* 41. In the episode, the pain in the foot was felt quite precisely along the line of this meridian. The sciatic pain Sophia had felt for years was on the same meridian, but in the thigh and the leg, not in the foot. It establishes an interesting continuity between the different episodes – they all happen along the same acupuncture meridian, but in different parts of it and with different modalities. This pattern is not uncommon; I have observed it in a number of clients. Some people seem to repeat ailments along the same meridian from one life to another.

This session brought further improvement, but it was only after a few more regressions that a final cure was achieved. Here is another important episode experienced by Sophia.

Where are you now? –I'm walking, I'm walking! I've left them and I'm going by myself.

Who are they? –The tribe. They wanted me to stay with them, but it did not feel right. It's me, but me in the future, not in this life. I've hesitated a long time, and they were putting pressure on me to stay with them. Like social pressure, the weight of habits and tradition. I had to stay with them and be like them, but then I dared to leave. I feel so free! I'm walking, I'm running along the hills and in a valley. Now that I have made my decision my leg feels completely free. I

> don't have to be like them. I can just be myself, whatever they think.
> I know I will never go back.

At the end of this ISIS process, Sophia's sciatic pain had completely disappeared, without any form of medical treatment, and it never reappeared. She could not only walk for hours in the bush, but also carry logs and take part in building projects. Yet surgeons had previously identified such damage from her spinal X-ray that they had given her a gloomy prognosis, even with surgery. This example shows how wrong it would be to believe that ISIS can only improve psychosomatic types of conditions, and not physical disorders.

6.5 No direct correspondence between physical disorder and samskara

So far, only examples with an obvious connection between the samskara and the physical disorder have been examined. Yet it is important to understand that in many cases, what is superimposed by the samskara is quite different from the original imprint. In other words, the pain or trouble generated by a samskara here and now may be of a different nature from that experienced when the samskara was contracted.

Case study – David, a thirty-four-year-old AIDS patient.

What are you feeling? –I'm falling in space. I don't have a body, I'm just in a dark space, falling.

Where does that take you? –Into a strange place. You go there before being born. You can see what is happening on the Earth from there. I can see how I am going to have to go into a womb and all that mess. I just do not want to go. I just want to stay there, in the space, but there is no real choice. I have to go but I don't want to. I don't want to go into the mess. I don't want to be born.

Have you sometimes felt the same thing, during your life? –I guess it's always been with me, in the background, the feeling of not wanting to be here.

Tell me, what's the difference between that feeling and a death wish? –I don't think there is much difference! Deep inside I know that the only way to get out of here is to die.

Do you mean that you have been living all these years with a death wish at the back of your mind? –Mm, yes, I guess so. [David laughed and then became very silent for a minute.]

The next step of the regression process would have been to find the source of the desire not to be on Earth, in other words the traumatic imprint from which the death wish originated. However, this was to be David's first and last regression. He had to be hospitalised before our next appointment, and died a few days later.

The 'I-don't-want-to-be-on-Earth' syndrome is far from rare. Regression shows that a large number of people carry such samskaric patterns with them, and only incarnate in their mother's womb with the greatest reluctance. In many cases, however, these patterns do not manifest as a death wish and do not create any major disease – only a lack of motivation and a reluctance to get involved in worldly occupations.

Let us be clear, I am *not* suggesting that regression can cure AIDS! If I were to draw any conclusion from this case study, it is that if a patient carries a major death wish, whatever the disease may be, I don't see how a final solution can be brought to the problem without dealing with the death wish, regardless of other treatments. Once an illness has appeared in the physical body, erasing the negative mental conditioning may not be enough to bring about healing. It is therefore quite sensible to use forms of therapy that will improve the physical state. But would a physical treatment by itself be enough? Is it reasonable to hope to cure a disease without dealing with its cause? And even if such a cure was possible, would it be a lasting one or just a palliative measure before the real problem reappeared somewhere else?

6.6 Can one heal a disease without treating its cause?

Primum non nocere, "First, don't make things worse," was an essential principle of Hippocrates' medicine. Nowadays, unfortunately, it seems to have been forgotten. Conventional modern medicine aims at getting rid of patients' symptoms. Little, if any consideration is given to the fact that some of these symptoms may actually be used by the body in an attempt to correct deeper disorders. When this is the case, suppressing the symptom does not necessarily help the patient. If the real cause (which may have nothing to do with the apparent symptom) is not dealt with, what happens to the patient once the symptom is 'cured'? This question is particularly relevant as far as samskara-related diseases are concerned.

Suppose a physical disorder is due to a samskara. The emotional charge of the samskara finds a temporary outlet through a physical symptom. Suppose the patient is given pills that kill the symptoms without dealing with the samskara. What will happen? The samskara will have to find a new outlet to express its emotional charge. This will manifest through other symptoms, either mental or physical, which may well end up being worse than the original trouble! Sooner or later, new disorders will appear, possibly with a much greater intensity, for the natural release of the emotional charge has been blocked. This means one does not necessarily help patients by getting rid of their symptoms, if one does not give them a chance to get in touch with the samskaras behind them. The following case study is typical of a medical history that could have gone on endlessly, had the samskara behind it not been neutralised.

Case study – Alexander is twenty-seven and has always been quite healthy, apart from an accumulation of problems all located in the same area: the right side of the abdomen. At the age of eight, he started suffering from recurrent pain in the right iliac area. One day the pain suddenly got acutely worse, and a surgeon decided that it was probably a case of appendicitis. Alexander underwent an operation for nothing, for the appendix proved to be perfectly normal. Yet, five days after the operation, the scar broke open again, and a second operation was needed. A big scar resulted, which worsened the problems of energy circulation in the area.

Five years later, exactly the same pain reappeared, but much more intense. This time all the surgeons agreed that it really looked like appendicitis – apart from the fact that the appendix had already been

---

cut out. Various tests were performed to try and find a cause, but without any success.

At the age of twenty-four, the young man went through violent attacks of renal colic, always on the right side. He even ended up passing a stone, confirming the diagnosis of lithiasis.

Even though the surgeons' diagnoses had changed with time, this young man had always felt that it was the same pain that kept coming back. The intensity was sometimes more, sometimes less, but the 'flavour' of the pain was exactly the same. The same 'flavour' was immediately identified when he reexperienced having been mortally wounded.

What are you feeling? –Despair. This time I'm not going to fight. I'm ready to die. I can see them coming. It's so easy, I just wait one little second instead of shooting. They shoot first. It feels as if I'm already out of my body, looking at the situation from above. I can see the man shooting, and the bullet travelling incredibly slowly, and reaching my body. The pain in my right side, it's my old pain, exactly the same. It pulls me back into my body, for a second. Everything becomes black. I can't see anything after that.

After four more regressions on the same episode the pains disappeared and never came back.

6.7 Samskaras and the genesis of disease

In this chapter, we have looked at a few examples of physical disorders that were caused by samskaras. This obviously leads to questions such as "Are all diseases due to samskaras?" and "Which diseases can be cured through regression?"

Our physical body is an extraordinarily well-constructed and durable instrument, considering we do not take much care of it, and that it usually takes more than half a century before we wreck it. In terms of robustness, not many of our technological achievements can compete. The body is also capable of many adjustments. For instance, one can live very well with only ten percent of one kidney, and one lung is plenty for a prosperous existence. For a disease to take place, it is usually not *one* single factor that is needed, but an accumulation of causes, some internal and some external.

It would be unreasonable, and a trifle dogmatic, to deny the importance of external factors in the genesis of disease. If your body absorbs more than a certain quantity of radiation, either from a man-made nuclear source or due to the depletion of the ozone layer, it is quite likely to manifest cancer. If you ingest certain toxins, you create irreversible body tissue injury, and so on. Nevertheless, it may be that several of these external factors reach you because you attract them. For instance we have seen how it is possible that accidents do not happen entirely by chance. We also know that when there is an epidemic, some people don't fall sick even though exposed to the germ. Clearly, certain individual factors greatly modify your sensitivity to external causes of disease.

It would be extremely difficult to try to determine in a scientific manner the part played by samskaras in the origin of diseases. Let's face it, nowadays, in the sphere of biology and psychology, something is declared scientific if it works on rats and if one can produce statistics about it. In that respect, rats do have samskaras. And one could probably do statistics on regression. But there is an obvious need for new models of understanding in the field of life-sciences in order to grasp why different individuals may react so differently to similar external conditions. The material emerging through regression certainly brings many elements in order to answer this question. From what we have seen of samskaras, we can draw the following conclusions:

1) Some samskaras do create physical disorders, and not only 'functional' ones. All kinds of ailments may result from the influence of samskaras, from simple headaches to cancer.

2) Once a samskara has generated a physical disorder, the latter gains its own momentum and won't necessarily disappear just by dealing with the samskara. Therefore, it seems logical to implement any appropriate physical treatment that may be required. But treating physical disorders without dealing with the samskaras behind them won't solve the patient's problems; it may even make them worse.

3) In most cases, it takes quite a long time before a disease develops out of a samskara. For years, the disorder is purely functional, or there is just an 'uncomfortable feeling' somewhere in the

body, without any other symptoms. The earlier the problem is dealt with, the more chance there is that the physical disorder will be terminated just by releasing the samskara, without the need for any other treatment.

4) Feeling a 'spot' somewhere in your body does not indicate that a disease will one day arise in this particular area! Firstly, most samskaras never generate any disease or physical disorder. Secondly, if they do create some kind of ailment, the 'spot' where a samskara is felt in regression or in meditation is often located in a different area from the physical disorder.

The accumulation of samskaras in the astral body has reached a level that could easily be called 'collective neurosis'. Our society is sick with samskaras, and on the brink of disaster. By a systematic eradication of samskaras through regression, incalculable future problems – both mental and physical – can be avoided.

What kind of diseases can be cured by regression? As with most forms of healing, the efficiency does not depend so much on the type of disease, but on the type of patient. Regression does not require that you believe in past lives, but it does require an open mind and a certain determination to face problems instead of trying to escape them. Falling sick is a way many people use to avoid looking at the source of their inner conflicts. If this is the case, success can only come if the patient is ready to acknowledge and own the conflicts – and not everyone is ready to do that.

I have seen regression bring spectacular results in a vast range of physical disorders, from skin troubles to abdominal tumours, from bladder incontinence to certain forms of paralysis. I have witnessed many improvements that amazed fellow physicians or made them pretend nothing had happened, because the results were irreconcilable with their present understanding of disease. However, I would certainly not present regression as a panacea. For I have also seen it to be inefficient in bringing physical relief for many other patients suffering from exactly the same types of disease.

To conclude this chapter, it may be of interest to ponder on a simple fact I have observed over the years. When working with ISIS, the clients who seem to go through the most spectacular healings are usually those who do not use the technique for the purpose of healing themselves, but for knowing themselves.

CHAPTER 7

THE END OF SAMSKARAS

7.1 Turning snakes into ropes

A significant result of ISIS is to make you become aware of the presence and the action of samskaras. By understanding the mechanisms of samskaras and analysing your emotional behaviour, you will identify certain patterns. Then through ISIS a number of totally unsuspected samskaras will be revealed. Some traumatic imprints of your past will be brought back to your consciousness, and you will immediately be able to make connections with present emotions and conditioned behaviour. The simple fact of *seeing* how a wrong mechanism operates in your mind already does half the work of neutralising it. The samskara is still there, superimposing its emotions on your awareness – but you can *see* it happening, and therefore it becomes much less of a problem.

There are many reasons why this is so. When the source of a pain cannot be recognised, the pain automatically tends to be magnified. Suppose you are on a beach and you put on your shirt after swimming. Suddenly, you feel a stabbing pain in the left side of your chest. It is so intense that your breath is taken away and you have to sit down. Immediately you start thinking of a heart attack or some other terrible disease, and a chain of associations follows – hospital, health insurance, and so on. Despair takes over! Then one minute later, you suddenly realise that a wasp was trapped inside your shirt, and that the pain came from having been stung. This brings instant relief! The 'injury' is exactly the same, but your suffering drops by more than half. The reason is simple; a few seconds ago you had a heart attack, and now you have just been stung by an insect. Even though the cause of the physical pain is exactly the same, your suffering is greatly diminished.

A classic example from the Hindu tradition illustrates this pattern. It is a story told by many masters, from a text of Vedanta called the *Aṣṭavakra-Gītā*. This *Gītā* was named after the great sage *Aṣṭavakra* who was physically 'eight times crippled' (*aṣṭa* = eight, *vakra* = twisted), and yet was one of the great teachers of eternal bliss of his time. *Aṣṭavakra* used the example of a snake that creates a big turmoil at a meeting. When the snake is discovered, the crowd is panic-stricken; everyone starts screaming and running in all directions. Then someone suddenly finds out that the snake is not a snake, but a coiled rope! Immediately, the agitation stops. Everything goes back to normal, and the people start laughing at their own reactions.

Each time you are afflicted by an emotion, the fact of seeing the samskara behind it completely changes your perspective, as when the snake becomes a rope, or as when the heart attack turns into an insect bite. It is not your boss or your boyfriend who is being cruel, it is not the world that is deliberately trying to hurt you. It is just a little mechanism inside that is playing its prerecorded message. It is a samskara, and nothing more.

However, a mere intellectual understanding of these processes is not going to help you much. A person trying to apply these principles without the direct experience of regression (or some other metaphysical way of consciously exploring deeply-rooted samskaric imprints) would be similar to a man who, facing a snake, tries to convince himself, "It is not a serpent, it is a rope". The whole enterprise would turn into a mockery. What you need is to be able to *see* the samskaras and reconnect with them consciously, which is exactly what ISIS allows you to do. For the 'magic' (*māyā*) of the samskaras is such that one may cheat oneself, but one cannot cheat them. As long as you do not *see* that the snake is a rope, the rope will bite you just as violently as the serpent would. It is by practising a technique such as ISIS and watching your reactions during your daily activities that you will move towards freedom, not by reading books about the topic.

The example of the snake and the rope also allows you to understand why young children are so vulnerable to emotions. Their logical mind is not yet developed. When something happens to them, they have no way of rationalising – no protective barriers; therefore, each time they come to mistake a rope for a snake, there is no way of getting them to see reason. The situation may be quite harmless, but to them it is as if their life was threatened. They can only panic, as you would do if you were attacked by some unknown beast in the middle of the night and had no way to escape or defend yourself. This explains why minor circumstances can create major samskaras in young children.

7.2 Samskaras are ridiculously small

There is another reason why seeing samskaras automatically neutralises a great deal of suffering; no matter how big the emotions arising from them may be, the samskaras themselves are nothing more than tiny seeds, ridiculously small compared to the upheavals they generate in your consciousness. Impulses arising from samskaras are artificially amplified by the astral body, as when an image is endlessly reflected by a set of mirrors. Were it not for this mechanism, emotional upheavals simply could not happen, or at least, they would never reach the same intensity.

The ISIS techniques aim at reaching a direct perception of the samskaras as seeds in the astral body. Before you can be shaken by anger or any other emotion, a wave has to arise from a samskara. Let us refer back to the sequence we previously described: stimulus → samskara → reaction/emotion.

At the core of our method of regression is the ability to perceive the waves of emotion coming out of the seed, or samskara. This requires the development of new qualities. To begin with, you must learn to perceive how samskaras make themselves felt in your body of energy. This is one of the first results from practising ISIS – you clearly feel your samskaras as 'spots' in various parts of your body of energy. This perception is neither vague nor ethereal, but as tangible as that of heat when putting your hand close to a fire. Suddenly samskaras stop being theoretical, you can feel them for yourself.

Another essential quality that needs to be developed is a certain awareness during daily activities. Whatever your method of spiritual development may be, without the cultivation of awareness nothing decisive can happen. If you try to work on your samskaras without watching them when they manipulate you, the fight is lost in advance. A key part of the process is to watch your own reactions in various situations in your life.

This does not mean that you have to suppress your emotions. This method does not ask you to stop being angry, yelling at your friends, or breaking plates. But while going through these daily routines, what you *have* to do is to be aware, meaning to watch yourself getting emotional and to feel the samskara behind the emotion. Persistent vigilance is required during your daily activities. In this awareness work, you do not need to see why and how the samskara originated. You do not need to reexperience the episode during which it was imprinted. All you need is to feel the seed of the samskara in your body of energy – the spot – and to sense the emotional wave coming out of it.

This process does not require special gifts or supernatural perception, but it does require strong perseverance. It implies that hour after hour, minute after minute, you watch your reactions to people and situations. If you persist in this direction, you will gradually become able to see the emotional waves at earlier and earlier stages of their emergence out of the samskaras – a great achievement. You will then discover that between the triggering of the angry samskara and the moment when you start breaking plates, there is quite a long way to go. The problem is that, if you had not done the work of awareness, all the reactions leading from the triggering of the samskara to breaking the crockery would have taken place extremely quickly, without you noticing anything. By systematically watching your reactions, you become aware of a number of intermediary stages during which the emotion is artificially amplified.

A great discovery is that the emotional wave, if you can see it as it first comes out of the samskara, is unexpectedly tiny. It is just a little vibration, it has hardly any emotional flavour attached to it. Then it takes all the magic (*māyā*) of your astral body to over-amplify this micro-vibration into a proper emotion, and to make you react and do all sorts of things that you would never choose to do if moved only by your own free will. Moreover, a lot of this amplification is not even due to what is related to the samskara itself; it is due to a kind of habit of your astral body. The astral body magnifies emotional vibrations; it is the way it has been conditioned to operate. Also, everything happens so quickly, you do not even realise that it is happening.

The situation becomes quite different if you systematically practise being aware. Each time the emotion takes place, you can see it evolving, phase after phase. You can even anticipate each phase while the process is happening: "I'm feeling the spot of the samskara, so I know I'm going to feel the vibration coming out of it soon. Now I'm feeling the vibration, and I know it is going to grow. Now the vibration has grown, so I know I am going to start feeling the emotion. That's it, the first hue of anger is appearing in my mind. Now it is growing, I can feel the anger vibration reaching my blood and flowing through it; just a bit more to go and I'll start yelling. That's it, I'm yelling and trembling. I'm going to start throwing the plates soon."

Of course, once your awareness has become that refined, it is highly unlikely that you will reach the stage of throwing the plates so readily. **Under constant observation, many repetitive emotional patterns become so unbearable that they end up dropping.** You see yourself always reacting the same way: "Now I'm going to feel that again. And then I'm going to say the same words, once more. And then I'm going to do that again", and so on. If you realise you have been carried away by destructive emotions only after they have happened, there is not much you can do about it. If you become aware while it is happening, the situation is quite different.

Another important outcome of being aware is that certain mechanisms of amplification by the astral body simply cannot take place. Let us look again at the diagrammatic representation of the subtle bodies we introduced in Chapter 4.

The stimulus is received through the senses of the physical body, transmitted through the etheric body, and reaches the astral body. Then the action of the samskara is to make the impulse bypass the layer of self-awareness. A chain of reactions takes place inside your astral body, which corresponds

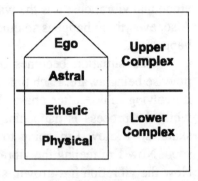

to the amplification mechanisms we have just described. If, however, the layer of self-awareness is not bypassed, then the scheme becomes completely different. The astral body loses its supremacy, and much of its 'chemistry' is automatically neutralised by the light of the Higher Ego. This means that if your self-awareness is strong enough, then the mechanical reactions of the astral body fall flat, automatically. **The weak point of the astral body is that it can operate freely only if you are unaware.** The more self-aware you become, meaning the more you involve the vehicle at the top of our diagram when receiving sensations and perceptions from the world, the less the astral body can manipulate you like a puppet. The leadership of the Self takes over and the power of conditioning drops.

It must be stressed again that, in this process, no suppression is implemented. If some emotions stop occurring, it is not because you are doing anything to block them. It is because their *māyā* has fallen away. Anyhow, what is the value of an emotion that vanishes as soon as you become aware of it? If an emotion disappears just by looking at it, it cannot be very real. This is another way of understanding the difference between emotions and feelings. **When a feeling arises inside you, the more aware you are, the stronger the feeling becomes. When an emotion arises, the more aware you are, the quicker it tends to vanish.** If you can *experience* this yourself over and over again, the illusory and artificial nature of reactional emotions will become so clear that your views on what is real or unreal in your psyche will change completely.

Let us try to understand more precisely the difference between clear vision and suppression, as far as emotional waves are concerned. When an emotion arises from a samskara, it is quite tiny and harmless. The stronger the awareness of the Self, the less it is possible for this minute vibration to blossom into a major reaction with adrenalin discharge, etc. It just remains as it is, and fades away. Instead of turning into an elephant, it remains the size of a cockroach. Suppression corresponds to quite a different mechanism: the vibration blossoms into an emotion, anger for instance, and then you hide the anger instead of expressing it. The main problem is that the anger energy is likely to play the kind of havoc inside you that Vedantic masters would compare to that of a mad elephant in your backyard.

7.3 Reaction versus awareness

The scheme we have just described suggests that at any stage of the development of an emotional wave you can either react or be aware, but not both. There are times when you are not aware and the reactions run their course mechanically. But when you are aware, the chain reaction stops. The original vibration arising from the samskara does not blossom into a fully-matured emotion, it gently dissipates. Of course in the beginning, the situation isn't always so clear-cut. In a number of cases you are aware that you are reacting, but even though you are aware, the chain reaction still follows its course to a certain extent, and reactional emotions still take place.

In this process, there is a conflict between two different parts of yourself: on the one hand, self-awareness, and on the other hand, the astral body and its automatic responses. The more the light of the Self shines in your self-awareness, the more it neutralises the wrong chemical reactions generated by your astral body. Yet there is a vicious circle, because it is precisely the samskaras which prevent the light of the Self from shining! So the process of liberation is twofold: on the one hand, reinforcing the awareness of the Self, and on the other hand, decreasing the power of the reacting mind by neutralising as many samskaras as possible. The first part corresponds to the various processes of meditation, initiation, rituals, and so on, while the second can be dealt with through ISIS.

In an over-simplified way, one could say that in the beginning of the work, consciousness consists only of the reactions of the astral body with no self-awareness. At the end of the work the self-awareness of the Higher Self radiates unobstructed, for the reactions of the astral body have been eradicated, and replaced by feelings. While accomplishing the work, various proportions of both self-awareness and reactions are present and interactive.

7.4 Releasing emotional charges

To weaken the grasp of the reacting mind, one thing will prove particularly potent – the release of the emotional charges associated with a limited number of extremely powerful samskaras. Some samskaras are endowed with devastating emotional energies, either because they were imprinted during dramatic circumstances – if you have been tortured, for instance, or if you have seen your children die in front of you – or because traumatic circumstances have hit you when you were especially vulnerable, as in the case of a young child who does not have the protection of a rational mind and magnifies some events out of proportion with their real nature. Those capital samskaras are stored with momentous emotional charges which raise the level of tension in the whole astral layer.

If you examine the way in which the reacting mind operates, you will see that everything in it responds to a law of polarities. A common point to all emotions is that they either attract you towards something, or repel you from it. An emotion is never neutral; it always has a polarity that pushes you in one direction or pulls you in another. This could be a good definition of an emotion: **an astral polarity that compels or repels**. From the point of view of the astral body, it is not the direction that matters, but the fact that there is a polarity, a charge. In simple words, to the astral body it does not fundamentally matter whether you love/desire someone or whether you hate/despise them. What matters is the intensity with which the inner charge is felt, and how irresistibly you are thrown into loving or hating.

This leads us to discern two distinct reasons why an emotion takes you over. Of course, there is the particular samskara that is triggered and reacts through the emotion; and behind this samskara there is a certain episode of your childhood, or your past lives, or both. Another essential reason, however, is also the general 'voltage' of your astral body. The more capital samskaras you have, the more their emotional charges will feed all your other samskaras and make them react violently. Consequently, as soon as you start releasing your capital samskaras, your emotional life becomes considerably simpler and much less out of control. This is because the general tension, the 'voltage' of the astral body drops significantly.

A further consequence is that an emotional problem can never be considered independently of the whole emotional layer. If you yell at your partner, it is probably not only due to the particular samskara related to this angry emotion, but also to several monsters of the depths. It is the charges of these mega-samskaras that feed your anger. Therefore only a global approach, dealing with the reacting mind as a whole, can bring real improvement.

As your vision expands you will come to realise that the situation is further complicated by the interactions with your environment. It is not only the emotional charges of your own capital samskaras that keep the voltage of your astral body artificially high, but also those of the people with whom you live and work. This influence should not be exaggerated, for it is active only within certain limits. Moreover, it is not healthy to blame your neighbours for your own moods. Spiritual history is full of people who reached metaphysical freedom in the most adverse circumstances. Nevertheless, the astral body is not as separate a layer as the physical body is, and it does receive emotional impulses and energies from our environment. Once more, this level of understanding should not be used as an excuse, and everyone remains responsible for the way they behave. For if your astral body was completely transformed, it would not be affected by disorganised collective astral waves. Yet this may give you clues as to why you may suddenly start feeling depressed or 'heavy' when certain world events causing widespread distress occur.

7.5 The metaphysical shift

Having discussed how necessary it is to cleanse the astral body and its many samskaras to reach freedom, it is now time to emphasise the reverse statement. If the work deals only with samskaras, it ends up going round in circles. If you focus only on emotions without ever experiencing higher states of consciousness, then you might well end up working on your emotions forever. This, of course, applies not only to regression, but to any form of psychotherapy or psychological exploration.

Regression

We have discussed how, if you meditate without dealing with your samskaras in a systematic way, there is a major risk of reaching a certain height and never being able to go beyond it, because you are tied to samskaras like a boat to an anchor. But if you do the opposite, if you work only on samskaras without meditating and developing higher states of consciousness, then you reach a certain depth of emotions and you stagnate. You clear some emotional blockages, you resolve some issues, and then you fall into a stalemate because your consciousness is lacking higher light to work more in depth. There is a correspondence between how high you can ascend and how deeply you can descend. As long as you are not in touch with higher qualities of consciousness, it is extremely difficult to reach the deepest layers of the astral body and its capital samskaras.

The problem is insidious because one can be completely blocked in one's progression and still have lots of emotional releases, which may give the false impression that one is advancing. You probably know some people in that situation. They get caught in some form of emotional therapy and never seem to be able to get out of it. They become better and better at expressing emotions, they can cry more and more, scream louder and louder. They keep on attending workshops in which they 'clear heaps'. But ten years later they are still working on similar emotional blockages, attending therapy workshops and 'clearing heaps' – nothing fundamental has changed in their life. This means that their work is purely horizontal. They explore more and more issues related to the same level of their mind, and are never able to go deeper.

When working on samskaras, one fact should never be forgotten – samskaras are endless! It is not by clearing more and more samskaras that one gets somewhere, but by clearing deeper and deeper ones, until one reaches the very source of all the graspings of the reacting mind. This *cannot* happen without regularly entering higher states of awareness of the Self, which usually implies some form of meditation. This applies not only to regression, but to any form of psychotherapy or psychological exploration. If a metaphysical opening does not take place at one stage, the process will go on forever without ever reaching a final resolution of the problems. Fundamentally, it is not on the emotional level that emotional problems can be solved, but through a metaphysical opening.

Consequently, for a real transformation of the psyche to take place, a strictly psychological form of work is insufficient. The more you incorporate a metaphysical dimension into the work, the more chances there are of a real breakthrough. A key point about the ISIS techniques is that they take you into various experiences of expansion of consciousness, of which reexperiencing past-life episodes is but a by-product. For example, the ISIS techniques allow you to travel far into the inner space and to peep into intermediary worlds, in which you have journeyed between death and birth. They also enable you to get in touch with angels and recognise the influence of various non-physical beings. All this creates an awakening of your spiritual vision. In order to understand what makes people change in the ISIS process, it is important to realise that the awakening of inner vision is at least as important as neutralising samskaras. Higher vision allows you to continue the process of psychological exploration in a vertical way. Instead of wandering endlessly around the same type of issues, it allows you to dive into the deepest layers of the astral body, and reach metaphysical experiences of the Self.

Of course the more emotional charges you can neutralise, the better. Clearing samskaras will bring definite improvements to all aspects of your life: physical, mental/emotional and spiritual. However, in itself, clearing samskaras is not enough. If you want to derive the most benefit from the ISIS regression techniques, it should be clear that their purpose is far greater than just dealing with samskaras. ISIS will take you on a number of journeys in your timetrack, and in different worlds and planes of consciousness. A deep maturation of your spiritual being and of your inner vision will result from these experiences. They will bring about as much change in you as the mechanical clearing of some samskaras, if not more.

As far as spiritual transformation is concerned, there is no direct causality. When dealing with day to day material tasks, you can draw up lists of problems and solve them one by one. As a result, your enterprises progress. You can see how solving each particular problem has helped you to advance. In spiritual work, however, progress is far from being so mechanical. There are problems and you work at clearing them, but real changes do not seem to come as a direct consequence of one particular process. You engage in various practices, and at some stage you realise that you have become different, and that a number of your past problems have disappeared. It is often impossible to pin-point when, how and why they have disappeared. You have gone through a deep maturation and you have become different, slowly. **You have shifted into a different quality of being, and in this new condition yesterday's problems simply can't be found anymore.** You realise that the problems you used to have were the consequence of how you were, more than anything else. Having become different, these problems are no longer with you.

7.6 The end of samskaras

What happens to samskaras after you have neutralised them through practising regression and awareness? They do not disappear, they remain as seeds. This is already a major improvement – there were twenty-four elephants in your loungeroom, and you turned them into twenty-four cockroaches. That is going to make life much easier. Yet, even though neutralised, the seeds remain; and even if they were to disappear completely, others would appear. Samskaras are like waves in the sea. 'Destroy' a wave and another one emerges, and so on forever. Samskaras are endless, and as we saw there is a very simple reason for this – the very nature of the manas/mind is to be 'samskared'. The very substance of the astral body is made of samskaras. Spending your life exploring one samskara after another cannot make sense.

The solution is of a different nature – shifting into a different layer of consciousness altogether. One cannot empty an ocean. One can make it somehow less murky by eradicating the main sources of pollution. However, the real answer to the problem is different – come out of the murky water and start existing in the open air. This means a shift of consciousness from emotions to feelings, or in other words from manas to *buddhi*, from the unaware consciousness of the astral body to the awareness of the transformed astral body (the Spirit-Self of Steiner's terminology), in which the Self radiates like a sun. This corresponds to an alchemical transformation through which the astral body is replaced by the transubstantiated astral body.

This transformation is gradual, and for a long period the reacting mind and its samskaras are still there, but they become less and less important. The reacting mind progressively loses its capacity to grasp you with its mechanistic routines. Your self-awareness grows in intensity and presence, up to the point where, being no longer obstructed by the reacting mind, self-awareness becomes awareness of the Self.

As the transformation takes place, you gradually lose your capacity for suffering. A beautiful gift you can hand to children is to help them learn the difference between pain and suffering. In the present human condition, pain is unavoidable. As long as you inhabit a physical body, you have to experience pain from time to time. Suffering is of a different nature. It is a reaction of the manas/mind that magnifies the pain and adds various emotional frills and thrills to it. In many cases, pain is only transient; but if one wishes one can always add to it and suffer more – there is no limit. This knowledge can easily be communicated to young children. For instance when they hurt themselves a little, mimic terrible suffering. Roll on the floor for fun, yell loudly, saying, "I suffer, I suffer" using all your melodramatic resources – they will get the message. The irony, of course, is that adults do the same all the time on another level, when they keep magnifying insignificant vibrations into huge emotions.

One of the lessons of ISIS is that even if pain is unavoidable, suffering is not; it can be completely eradicated. This is not a remote metaphysical ideal, but an achievable goal that you can reasonably set yourself, if you are prepared to put the method into practice with perseverance. If you combine ISIS with watching your reactions systematically, it won't be long before a substantial part of your suffering drops, having been exposed as unnecessary grasping of the mind.

CHAPTER 8

REMEMBERING PAST LIVES

8.1 Why don't we remember our past lives?

Before analysing the mechanisms by which past lives can be remembered, let us look at why most people, under usual circumstances, are unable to remember them.

Firstly, people are unable to remember most of their dreams. If they are not even able to remember their dreams, how could we expect them to remember their former lives? Fundamentally, the reasons for not remembering past lives are the same as those for not remembering dreams. To understand this situation fully, let us recapitulate a few details of subtle anatomy, that is, the knowledge of the subtle bodies that constitute the totality of a human being.

1) Everyone is familiar with the physical body – the one that surgeons can open and cut. As it is made of the nutrients we eat, the Vedantic tradition has called it *anna-maya-kośa*, the 'sheath-made-of-food'.[1]

2) Beyond the physical is the etheric body, made of vital energy which is the *Qi* of traditional Chinese medicine and the *prāṇa* of Sanskrit literature. Hence the name *prāṇa-maya-kośa*, 'envelope-made-of-*prāṇa*' given to this layer in Vedanta. Just as water permeates a sponge, so the envelope of *prāṇa*, or etheric body, penetrates the whole of the physical body.[2] It also extends a little beyond the limits of the physical body.

---

[1] *Anna* = food; *maya* = made of; *kośa* = sheath or envelope.

[2] The hardest substances of the physical body, mainly the bones, are not penetrated by the etheric as much as the soft tissues are.

As long as you are alive, your physical and etheric bodies never separate. Therefore we can regard the two of them as an individualised structure, which for our purpose will be called the 'lower complex'.

3) Beyond the physical and etheric bodies is the astral body, layer of the manas/mind, or reacting mind, in which emotions and most of our thoughts take place. As discussed earlier, the samskaras have their seat in the astral body.

4) The Ego is at the centre of all the other bodies. At a later stage, when dealing with more advanced alchemical processes, I will make clear distinctions between Ego, Self and Spirit. But in the context of this book, these distinctions would not be of any real use. So, to simplify, we can consider the words Ego (or Higher Ego), Self (or Higher Self) and Spirit as synonymous and referring to the immortal flame which is the core of human beings.

It is important to note that the astral body and the Ego are closely tied. One could even say that the Ego is tangled in the web of the astral body. That is why when you close your eyes, unless you have followed a path of self-transformation, you are not able to discriminate what in your consciousness comes from the mind and what belongs to the Self. You may know intellectually that you have a Higher Self, and that this Self is the background of your consciousness, like a white screen on which various movies are projected. But in practice the Self is hidden by the reacting mind, so that it is impossible for you to connect directly with its light. Therefore the first purpose of a spiritual path is to separate the Self from the astral body.

As long as this has not happened, to cite an analogy often found in Sanskrit literature, the two remain mixed like milk and water in the same glass. The astral body and the Ego are bound together. Consequently we can simplify our four-storey structure by splitting it into two:

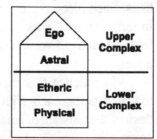

• an upper complex, made of the astral body and the Self, which do not separate as long as you have not 'found your Self';

• a lower complex, made of the physical and etheric bodies, which do not separate as long as you are alive.

8.2 Full of holes like a colander, or gruyere cheese

What happens when you sleep? The lower complex (physical body + etheric body) stays in bed, while the upper complex (astral body + Ego) departs and wanders into different spheres. The two complexes remain linked by what some esotericists call the silver cord. So the waking and sleeping states correspond to two different directions taken by the astral body. During the day the astral body cognizes the physical world through the physical senses of the physical body. During the night it withdraws from the physical body and directs its activity towards the various astral worlds, which results in dreams and other deeper states of consciousness. When it is time to wake up, the astral body leaves the astral sphere and re-enters the physical body.

The reason why we do not remember much of our dreams and other nightly astral activities is that in the present stage of human development, the astral body leaks like a colander. It is full of holes, like gruyere cheese. Moreover, the bridges of communication between the lower complex (physical body + etheric body) and the astral body are not properly developed. So even if the astral body can retain some of the night's experiences, the corresponding memories have little chance of passing through and reaching your waking consciousness.

In its present condition, the astral body is painfully lacking structure, and even more, lacking unity. It appears like a bunch of ill-matched patches. We could compare it to a jigsaw puzzle whose pieces do not fit with one another. Each piece of the puzzle has its own samskaras and its own emotions, desires, attractions and dislikes. Each piece corresponds to a different facet of your personality. In terms of past lives, each of these pieces has been wrought at different periods of your past, under the influence of various life experiences.

In practice this means that as a psychological being, you are made of parts, each with its own flavour, its own past and its own desires. For instance, a part of yourself may love to read books about spirituality, while another part is interested in gambling on the horses, and yet another in travelling around the world. Each of these parts is one of the multiple 'characters' that constitute your personality. The word character is quite appropriate, for in ancient Greek it meant a mark impressed, engraved or stamped, as on a coin or a seal – which fits very well with the mechanisms we have described about samskaras. In this context we could define a character as a bunch of samskaras imprinted on a particular piece of the astral body, and working at satisfying its own desires according to its own past.

The drama of life is that each of these characters works for itself and does not care about what the other parts want. For instance the part that loves gambling does not care about the wisdom described in the books your spiritual character hoards. So the interplay of the characters will often put you in painfully contradictory situations. Each character is like a potential dictator which aims at taking over your life and transforming it according to its own likes and dislikes. For example, the 'reader' in you wouldn't mind turning your house into a gigantic library, while the 'gambler' would love to see you get a job as a sports reporter. The only common interest shared by the characters is to alienate your Self as much as possible, because if the Self was to start ruling, it would mean the end of any possible supremacy for them. Consequently the reality of life for most people is that the Self is anaesthetised and kept dormant in the background, while different characters fight for rulership.

8.3 The exploded mosaic

What happens when you die? The upper complex (astral body + Ego) separates from the lower one (physical body + etheric body), just as when you fall asleep. But this time the silver cord is broken, and the lower complex is abandoned. The physical body starts to rot, and the etheric body disintegrates into the global etheric layer of the planet. It would be inaccurate to believe that the upper complex will go and travel in

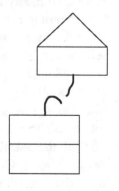

spiritual worlds and come back just as it is for a new incarnation, after perhaps a bit of cleansing and a few improvements made by angels.

The reality of the situation is dramatically different. When most people die, their astral body is turned into chaos, due to the lack of unity we have described. The multiplicity of the characters is not only functional; it reflects the fact that the very structure of the astral body is a mosaic, or patches artificially kept together as long as you are alive. When the time of death comes, this illusion of unity is dispelled. The facade of the personality falls and the astral body is experienced for what it really is – an exploded mosaic.

Practically, this means that soon after the silver cord is broken, most of the astral bits are going to fly away, each in their own direction, like birds escaping when you open their cage.

For the person who has just died this is quite a dramatic experience. Picture yourself dead, floating in the purple astral space. You see your 'reader' character move away from you in one direction, the 'gambler' in another, the part of yourself that could speak Japanese in another... You are literally stripped, dismembered. The parts that were more related to enjoyment, sexuality and instincts move towards the vital worlds, while your mental parts depart for the mental worlds – and what is left? Your Ego, or Higher Self, with a few remnant shreds of astral body. Then the stripped Ego can start its journey into the worlds of the Spirit.

This explains what Gurdjieff meant when he said that for the great majority of human beings, it does not make any sense to talk about reincarnation, simply because they do not have an astral body. More than ninety-nine percent of human beings have an astral body that is nothing more than a bunch of butterflies. Of course these people will reincarnate, but what exactly will reincarnate? Their Higher Self, which is precisely the part of themselves they never became aware of during their life, and which took virtually no part in their activities. Nearly everything they used to consider as 'themselves' will disintegrate and return to astral dust. It is no wonder they will not be able to remember much in their next life, since they have lost most of the astral substance in which the impressions of this life were recorded. Gurdjieff sharply summarised this situation by saying, "The dust returns to dust".

8.4 White as the real colour of mourning

Unfortunately, all astral bits do not return to astral dust. Many of them tend to remain as they are and stick to living human beings to try and perpetuate their activity.

This explosion of the astral body is why the traditional Hindu custom was to wear only white and perform a semi-fast, avoiding mainly proteins, during the weeks following the death of someone in their family. The Hindus consider that some of the lower vital parts of the dead may try to stick to other members of the family in a parasitic way. Wearing white, the colour of purity, and avoiding meat and grains, are regarded as protective measures to diminish the possibility of such 'bugging'.[1] The custom is still observed, even in modern and educated parts of India.

A very similar theory can be found in traditional Chinese lore. The *Po*, corresponding to lower vital parts of a human being, is said to remain on the Earth after death, while the *Hun*, made of the more spiritualised parts, ascends to heaven. The *Po* can even appear to family members or friends as a frightening replica of the dead, in the hours or days after the latter has passed away. The parallel with a number of ghost stories is obvious. A detailed analysis of these mechanisms can be found in my book, *Entities, Parasites of the Body of Energy*.

8.5 Forgetfulness due to lack of presence

Let us now focus on the part that is not annihilated. The Self, or Ego, being the eternal flame in a human being, remains untouched while going through the transition of death. The question is, of course, what else persists? What are the mechanisms by which some astral parts are lost, while others remain attached to the Self and follow it in its journey between death and the next birth?

---

[1] White appears white to our eyes because it reflects all the frequencies of the visible spectrum. Keeping nothing and reflecting everything, white has universally been attributed with a symbolism of purity. Black, reflecting nothing and keeping everything, is the absorbing colour par excellence, and therefore the worst possible colour to wear in situations such as funerals, where there is a high risk of catching negative energies.

The matter is of importance, for the astral parts that persist and accompany the Self will be the core of your personality in the following life. After death, the Ego passes through various astral layers, and then departs to the Spirit worlds. After staying in these worlds, it returns to the Earth via the astral worlds. It is while passing through the astral layers on its way back to the Earth that the Ego collects the matter of its future astral body. The astral parts that the Ego had kept around it act as a core, gathering astral substance according to their own dispositions – which will result in likes and dislikes, as well as emotional and mental potential in the following life. So whatever remains attached to the Ego after death conditions what we will be in our next life.

Before trying to understand how some memories can be kept in the central astral core around the Ego, let us first see how most are lost. While performing the great majority of the actions in their life, people are totally unaware. We tend to go through our daily activities mechanically. We talk without real purpose. We do things without even knowing that we do them. We are not really present to what we are doing. Even if we practise being aware, entire portions of our days can elapse before we retrieve our thread of awareness. In short, we are not living our life, we are sleeping it.

In terms of subtle bodies, this means that the Ego does not take any part in these actions. Sensory perceptions are received in the astral body, in the pieces of the astral puzzle. Then these pieces react mechanically according to their own likes and dislikes, meaning their own samskaras. Reactional actions are performed more or less mechanically, and the Ego is bypassed. Everything remains in the periphery of the astral layer. Nothing is imprinted close to the Ego, simply because the Ego is absent from the episode. How can the Ego remember the episode if it is not involved in it? Here lies the main reason for the forgetfulness of the Spirit: unawareness. In terms of astral imprint, there is nothing more than dust, which will later return to dust.

8.6 Remembrance type 1 – intensity

There are a few situations where this scheme of forgetfulness does not apply. Suppose you are lying on a riverbank and a crocodile appears out of the blue and rushes at you. It is quite likely that you are going to be very aware for a moment. Imagine... The whole of yourself gets involved in the situation, you are *totally present*. Any emotions you may feel, together with sensations and perceptions, are impressed in the deepest layers of your astral body. The climax of awareness indicates that your Ego emerges from its slumber for a while. There is a breakthrough of the Ego into the physical world and simultaneously, a breakthrough of information into your deepest astral layers. A whole package of perceptions, sensations and emotions is stored close to the very core of your inner architecture. The track left in your astral body by such an 'emotional package' can indeed be regarded as a major samskara. Due to the depth of the imprint, all the conditions are gathered for you to keep the corresponding astral fragment with your Ego, even after the stripping at death, and bring it back with you in your next life.

So the first category of past-life remembrance is made of various experiences which share one common feature – intensity. Extremely painful experiences can be related to this category. Whenever you experience a climax of physical or emotional pain, you automatically become acutely aware. Pain, however, is not necessary for intensity. For example, if you see land appearing in the distance after crossing the Pacific on a raft, or if you suddenly succeed in getting what you want after years of effort, the intense elation of the moment will secure a deep imprint, the source of possible future recollections. This is of course why many past-life regressions unveil intense episodes.

8.7 Remembrance type 2 – spontaneous openings

From time to time, without any reason in the external world, the Higher Self breaks through and opens to the surface. A spontaneous and temporary awakening takes place. It can be experienced as an inner revelation, one of those rare, clear moments when one can see forever. One sits at a crossing of time, with an intuitive feeling of one's eternal nature and vastness. But the experience does not have to be grandiose, it can simply be a magic moment, a few seconds during which the heart explodes with causeless joy. Then the sanctuary closes again, because our whole structure is not ready to maintain the connection.

During this moment of opening, a link has been established between the surface and the deepest, between the consciousness of the physical world and the awareness of the Higher Self. The necessary conditions are fulfilled for an imprint deep enough to last beyond the astral shattering after death. The circumstances, feelings, sensations and perceptions of such a moment are memorised beyond time.

8.8 Remembrance type 3 – the body of immortality

The constant practice of vigilant awareness, which is the basis of many paths of self-transformation, tends to multiply the occasions when the Higher Self involves itself in daily life. This results in multiplying the seeds for future remembrance.

In former chapters we have outlined the transformation that leads from emotions to feelings, from manas to *buddhi*, from reaction and conditioning to the spontaneity of the Ego. This gradual metamorphosis goes with the development of a new layer, a 'transformed astral body' called Spirit-Self by Steiner, and which corresponds to the *vijñāna-maya-kośa* of the Vedantic tradition. The astral body, seat of the samskaras, loses its predominance and is progressively replaced by this new layer in which the Ego expresses itself directly. In parallel with the replacement of emotions by feelings, a new mode of thinking emerges that is no longer disconnected from the Ego, but radiates from it. The development of the transformed astral body corresponds to the blossoming of a new inner consciousness directly connected with the Higher Self.

Another major difference between the astral body and the transformed astral body is that the astral body is made of separate parts constantly trying to escape the rulership of the Ego. The transformed astral body on the contrary is united around the Ego, completely permeated by its light and its life. It can't be separate from the Ego, for it is none other than the Ego's radiation. The astral body is made of coagulated astral dust, whereas in the matter of the transformed astral body, the Spirit itself is alive. The substance of the transformed astral body can virtually be regarded as *Self-ness*. The Self generates it as the spider secretes its web.

Consequently the transformed astral body remains intact after death, while the astral body is shattered. Therefore the memories

104

stored in the transformed astral body are kept forever. So from the point of view of structure, we can discern two different types of past-life material: the samskaras that were imprinted so deeply in the astral body that they keep hanging around the Self from life to life; and the memories of the transformed astral body which persist in the imperishable substance of the body of immortality.

Yet the situation is not so clear-cut, because there is a long transition period during which consciousness operates partly in the astral body and partly in the transformed astral body, the proportions depending on your level of development. Structurally this results in an astral web made of tangled patches of these two vehicles. Some memories are stored in both the astral body and the transformed astral body, or even half in one, half in the other.

Let no one be confused; as far as the vast majority of human beings are concerned, the transformed astral body remains a remote ideal. The mechanisms of past-life remembrance through the body of immortality do not apply, simply because the transformed astral body is not built. Only people who in this life or in former ones have followed a long process of development, have acquired rudiments of transformed astral body. In the great majority of cases when a past-life experience takes place it is through the imprints left by the samskaras, as described in the section, 'Remembrance type 1 – intensity'.

CHAPTER 9

THE WAY TO RECOVERING MEMORIES

9.1 Breakthrough into past-life memories

Having analysed the ways some memories are kept from one life to another, let us now look at the problem from the other end; through which mechanisms can one recover some of these memories? How can one remember elements about one's past lives?

If there is an inner sanctuary where the memories of our remote past are to be found, then this place is beyond our daily waking consciousness.

The conscious life of most people is confined to the 'talking mind', the most superficial layers of the astral body. Remember the path followed by the Ego after death: having cast off most of the patches of the astral body, it journeys through various astral layers, and then into the Spirit worlds. Then the Ego returns to the astral worlds, gathering astral matter around itself. The astral core that persists after the shattering plays a key role in what type of astral material is gathered. The transformed astral body, or even the beginning of it, could play an even greater role in structuring a harmonious astral body. Unfortunately, in the vast majority of human beings, the transformed astral body is barely developed and only plays a negligible part. So it is the hard core of the samskaras from past existences that plays the dominant role in attracting the astral matter of our next astral body. This hard core is very tiny indeed, and surrounds itself with a number of layers.

After birth you gradually learn to use your mind, meaning you experience thoughts and emotions in your astral body. But this happens mainly through external stimulation. The superficial layers of the astral body are moulded from outside by your education and all that you receive from your parents and your culture. In the superficial layers of the astral body, you operate with the elements received from the outside world. This results in a polarity in the astral body, a tension between the deep impulses coming from the impressions brought from past lives, and the impressions collected in this life. A great part of your mental abilities, artistic sensitivity, emotional stability and other qualities depends on how harmoniously the marriage takes place between inner and outer impulses, that is, between the material you brought with you and that which you accumulate in this present life.

The surface layer, meaning your conscious mind, is constantly influenced by emotions and various reactions coming from the samskaras of the depths. But it never sees these samskaras, because the buffer zone is too thick.

If you want to remember your past lives, you need to dive into the deepest layers of the unconscious mind. This requires an energy that allows you to break through and reach the parts of the astral body close to the central core of the Self – the parts in which past-life memories are inscribed. This breakthrough energy makes all the difference between regression and other techniques of psychotherapy. Why does psychoanalysis not lead to past-life regressions? Simply because psychoanalysts lack this breakthrough energy. Why did so many initiates, Christian Gnostics, Hindus and Buddhists remember their past lives? Because having found their Self, they had access to the breakthrough energy and the material inscribed close to the Self. Why is regression much easier to reach now in the nineteen-nineties than in the late seventies, and why is it spreading quickly? Because due to an awakening in collective consciousness, the breakthrough energy is far easier to access than it used to be.

The fact that the regression state comes from this energy explains why, once familiar with the ISIS techniques, you have to do very little to regress a client; the energy does the work through you. For the same reason, you need to know very little to be a good connector. What you need is to be able to tune in and let the force act through you. If you know a lot, then you have to forget all you know. All the information required to conduct a good regression is contained in the energy, and if you try to apply what you know rather

107

than what the energy dictates, the results will be mediocre and you will often miss the most important issues.

It also explains why, after you have conducted a number of ISIS sessions, your clients will often start regressing even before you begin implementing the techniques. The energy flows through you like a living stream, it does not care about techniques.

Who are good subjects for regression? Those who can connect with this energy, who can open and receive it, whether young or old, healthy or sick. It does not matter whether they believe in past lives or not, provided they can be open. Some great disbelievers prove able to connect immediately, while some people who believe too much in reincarnation tend to build up expectations that block the flow of energy. Their preconceptions leave no space for the energy to work.

9.2 The flash of astrality

Since the samskaras are stored in areas of the astral body that lie beyond the usual field of your waking consciousness, it follows that for past-life remembrance to take place, a link has to be established between the conscious mind and these deep layers of the astral body.

Certain signs indicate when this connection has been made. For instance, a special feeling arises in the room. The 'atmosphere' changes completely, as if a flash of astral energy had been brought down around you. If you have practised the techniques indicated in *Awakening the Third Eye*, you may be familiar with some of the other signs. In particular, the room suddenly appears darker to your eye. In this darker space, the colours look more luminous, as if each colour was actually made of thousands of tiny shining points. Of course it is not the room that becomes dark, but your perception that opens to the 'darkness visible' superimposed on the light of the room. You can also sometimes feel a characteristic sensation in the kidneys, due to the intense connection of these organs with the astral body.

Even if you are not familiar with these signs, you can easily learn to recognise the 'flash of astrality' that accompanies the regression state. The energy in the room suddenly becomes 'denser'; and the 'flavour of consciousness' becomes somewhat similar to that of the dream state. (Remember how you feel when waking up just after a dream.) This does *not* mean that regression and dreams are similar! The two states are quite different. Yet both involve a redirection of consciousness towards astral layers, which explains why their 'flavours' are related.

9.3 The content of past-life memories

From the mechanisms of past-life remembrance we analysed in the last chapter, we can draw a few conclusions about the content of past-life memories. Of course, we must keep in mind that we are dealing with a field which is beyond the ordinary aspects of existence, and therefore in which one should not generalise too quickly. With regression, virtually anything is possible! Let us therefore not presume that all past-life regressions will necessarily follow the patterns indicated below. Still, a clear understanding of certain mechanisms will allow connectors to be more helpful to their clients. Ignorance of these principles may lead to gross mistakes that cause the regression state to abort in the first minutes of the experience.

Let us go back to the example of the fierce crocodile that suddenly rushed at you in a former life. What exactly will be stored in the astral body? The content of your mind at that moment, starting with the fear, of course, and the whole emotional atmosphere around it – we could say the 'flavour' of the situation – the thoughts that came to you, and all the perceptions and sensations of the instant: the colours of the landscape, the smells of the marsh, the feeling of heat, the contact of your clothes and the wind on your skin... a movie-like recording of these instants with the most minute details, outside and inside you.

Now, what has *not* been stored? All the elements of your life that were not in your mind at that precise moment. Your address, for instance, or the date, the name of the country, even your name. For the first reflex, when confronted by a crocodile, is not to say, "It is 1854, I am in Africa, my name is Wolfgang and I am an explorer".

Another thing that is not stored is the judgments you may have made later, such as, "How brave I was!" or "How stupid I was!" or "I could have done this differently". All these judgmental comments could not be recorded in the 'movie', because they came later on.

The recording process can be compared to a plane's black box, which registers all the parameters at a critical moment.

9.4 The art of giving birth

So a genuine past-life remembrance is usually very simple. It is a package of emotions, sensations, feelings and images related to a particular moment – the moment when the pressure of the emotion made your Self 'reopen'. Everything has been precisely recorded and stored, and the client reexperiences the scene exactly as if the crocodile was in front of him. His body can even take the same attitude as in the scene, and all the emotions and sensations are recalled as if they were happening here and now.

Yet reexperiencing the episode is far from being traumatic, for the client remains perfectly conscious of who he is now, of the room in which the session is being conducted, of the mattress on which he is lying, of the connector's voice, and so on. Moreover, whenever the ISIS state is reached, a certain metaphysical opening takes place which adds a background of great serenity to the experience, however intense the episode may be. Also, to the client, the emotional charge of the samskara was a heavy burden, and therefore reexperiencing the past trauma is accompanied by a great feeling of relief, as if poison was being eliminated.

Let us go back to the way the client enters the regression experience. In some extreme cases the whole scene will flash back in one second, with all the details. But in most cases, all the components of the scene do not come back at the same time. The beginning of the experience is gradual, with only a few details arising in the client's consciousness. For instance the client has a glimpse of an emotion and tells the connector, "I'm afraid" or "I hate this person". Or maybe the experience starts with a sensation such as feeling cold, and the client starts shivering, even on a hot summer's day. Or the client says, "I'm being kicked in the ribs" or "There is a heavy weight on my shoulders". These first impressions are often faint. They are the first thread that has to be followed carefully in order to gradually recover more and more elements of the scene, until the full tableau is unveiled.

The connector faces a delicate task; a misunderstanding of the mechanisms of remembrance may lead him or her to ask clients the wrong questions, possibly resulting in losing the thread instead of stepping more firmly into the regression state. At this stage the clients are drifting between two states of consciousness: the usual waking state, and the regression state. They are only perceiving a few sensations or details of the scene. They need some help to enter the regression state more deeply, and it is the connector's function to provide this help, by asking certain questions. But the questions will have to be carefully chosen.

Suppose the connector asks, "What is your name?" or "Which country are you in?" Clients will only be confused, for at this stage they do not have the faintest memory of such details. They are not seeing even ten percent of the scene yet. So how could they know what country it was? As discussed before, when being attacked by a crocodile one does not usually ponder upon geographical considerations. From the state they are in, clients simply cannot answer such questions – these details are beyond their reach. So what will happen? In order to find an answer, clients will have to think, meaning go back into their usual mental consciousness. In one second they will be out of the regression state, and the experience will be lost. For the same reasons, at this fragile stage if clients cannot answer one of your questions, do not insist; ask another one. Later on, when clients are firmly established in the regression state, the situation will be quite different; if no answer is given to a question, it is more likely to be due to a mechanism of resistance, and the connector must insist.

In the first minutes of a regression, the right questions are those which bring an immediate and effortless answer. They refer to elements that are within reach of the client, even though he is not fully aware of them yet. For instance, "How does your body feel, big or small?" or "How does it feel around you, warm or cold?" To answer, the client does not have to think, but just to feel. In this way you allow him to penetrate further into the scene by gradually adding more elements, until he sinks fully into reexperiencing the episode. Altogether, the process is not so different from giving birth.

9.5 Examples of successful sinking

These mechanisms do not only apply to the remembrance of past-life episodes, but also to scenes of early childhood, as shown in the following example.

Case study – Simone, aged fifty-two.

The beginning of the session was painful and agitated, as if Simone was pregnant with the experience but unable to let it out. After half an hour of work – should we say labour? – the atmosphere suddenly changes in the room, and all the above-mentioned features of the flash of astrality can be sensed.

What are you feeling now? –I don't know, I just feel very strange. [At this stage, the client cannot see anything of the episode. But the experience is close, hence the strange feeling.]
Does it feel more like being male or female? –Mm... Neither male nor female. [This question is premature and does not really help to engage the process.[1] But the following ones make it click.]
Does it feel more like day or night? –Night.
Does it feel like being big, or small? –Little, little... empty... all alone... [Simone curls up and crosses her arms against her chest. She is one step further into the experience, but everything is still blurry. Through the following questions the situation starts to appear clearly to her.]
What do you want? –My mother! I want my mother!
Is she with you? –No! No! No! I'm hungry and nobody is feeding me. [Simone starts crying with huge sobs, sucking her thumb. From there she can see all the details of the scene: the furniture in the room, the colour of the curtains, etc. From this point on the regression unfolds more or less by itself.]

---

[1] When contacting an experience related to early childhood, it is quite common for clients to find it difficult to decide whether they are male or female.

112

Case study – Twenty-seven-year-old man. At the beginning of the session, a very painful spot is revealed under his left shoulder blade. After working on the spot for a few minutes, the energy starts changing in the room. The pain disappears, and the client becomes very quiet.

What are you feeling? –[No answer. Everything is still extremely blurry.]

How does your body feel, big or small? –Big.

Does it feel like you are moving or motionless? –Motionless.

In which position? –Lying on my back. On a bed.

Do you feel young or old? –Old. [All these answers come out immediately and effortlessly, without thinking. The tone of the client's voice gradually changes, indicating that he is starting to feel surer of what he senses. The click comes after the next question.]

Healthy or sick? –Tired, very tired. It is like I am going to die... and accepting it. It has been good! But at the same time I feel angry. [The client has completely entered the episode and from now on stays in it.]

Is there any reason for this anger? –I was going to tell my son something.

Like what? –I was going to tell him that I love him. It feels like my life has been wasted, because I could never tell him that I loved him.

Does it feel as if you are alone, or with someone around you? –I'm not alone, there are some spirits around me.

What do they look like? –Friendly. They know me. They're around my body and they're waiting for me to die completely. They are saying, "You've gone through this before". They're like friends that you've not seen for a while. But I want to talk to my son.

9.6 The metaphysical opening

Once clients are more firmly established in the regression state, all sorts of questions can be asked. The way each sentence is weighted and formulated is still important for the session to continue properly, but there is far less risk of the experience being suddenly lost.

The content of the clients' consciousness while in the regression state is a strange melange in which past and present are superimposed on one another. The clients reexperience the episode as if it was happening right in front of them, feeling the corresponding emotions and sensations. It is like entering another body and being another person – yet this other person feels extremely familiar.

You can get a sense of this continuity when you recall how you felt as a very young child. That was quite a different 'you', but still there is an inner certitude, beyond any possible doubt, that it was yourself. During regression it is an extension of this experience that arises. You get the same inner certitude of your identity, even if the past-life 'you' is far more different from the present 'you' than the 'you' of early childhood. But it is still the same 'you'. This experience of identity is of a metaphysical nature and can't be fully understood as long as you haven't gone through it yourself.

So, during a regression, we have the superimposition of two 'you' – you in the past, and you in the present. For in the ISIS techniques of regression, no hypnosis is used, nor any device that would aim to diminish your present awareness. You remain fully aware of yourself now, and at any instant you can choose to disconnect from the regression state and be only aware of the room, your body, and the present 'you'.

The superimposition of the two 'you', past and present, is a most fascinating experience. For you have changed. The 'flavour' of your inner environment has become completely different. And yet it is the same you, there cannot be the faintest doubt. It does not matter how far back in time the episode may have taken place, whether hundreds or even thousands of years – the continuity of the Self is unaffected by time.

So here you are, standing at the crossing of times, suddenly realising that 'you' can be quite different from what you are used to. You suddenly become aware that you live your life in a matchbox. You realise that you tend to confine your existence within a limited range of emotions and feelings, always the same repetitive routines. At the same time you can see it doesn't have to be so, for you are infinitely vaster. The superimposition of the past you on the present you, allows you to peep into the incredible depth of your Self. It is a vastness without end, a motionless explosion. Suddenly you *are*.

This is the most central experience regression can give – and the most healing as well. Just a glimpse of your real nature can bring more change in your life than years of discussion and analysis of your problems. For ultimately, one does not get rid of problems by dealing with samskaras, but by stepping into the Self.

CHAPTER 10

FREQUENTLY ASKED QUESTIONS

10.1 Why focus on negative emotions, instead of working only on the light? Isn't it giving power to negative conditioning to spend energy looking at it? Why not just expand our light?

Suppose there is a dead rat rotting under your sofa. You can put a few nice blankets over the sofa, so nobody can see the rat. You can buy flowers and try to cover the stench with a lovely fragrance. Then each time you are in the room, you will focus on the lovely fragrance in order not to give power to the foul stench coming from the rat's corpse. But is that really a solution?

Another common attitude is to avoid that room from now on, and live only in the rest of the house. Many spiritual people proceed in this way; they build up more and more light in certain parts of themselves and leave a few dark corners without ever looking at them. The result is that the disparity between the clear side and the dark side keeps increasing, which cannot be completely satisfying. When some people follow a spiritual path and have the feeling that they are doing 'all the right things', and yet enlightenment never seems to come, it is usually because they have adopted this attitude.

Another problem is that human beings have reached a stage where there are dead rats in virtually every single corner of the house, which makes the ostrich attitude more and more difficult to sustain. You are left with only a tiny cupboard on the top floor, in which you can be 'fully enlightened'.

Or maybe you will choose the attitude of the ascetic. "This house is pure illusion; I have always hated it. I'll stand on top of the roof and never get back into this mess." Then you can be fully en-lightened on your roof, and not have to worry about the corpses in-

116

side the house. But then, that is it! You are dead to the world, you are out of it. The only thing you can do for other human beings is to teach them too how to leave the house and be enlightened on the roof.

The perspective of inner alchemy is different, it aims at transforming the vehicles of consciousness. It aims at an enlightenment *in* the world, not out of it. In that case you have to clean up the mess, you can't simply ignore it. You have to work at bringing the light into every single room of the house. It is unreasonable to expect this to happen until you take the trouble to move the sofa and get rid of the corpses.

10.2 Do we really need to go through regression to get rid of samskaras? After all, many Hindu masters have reached enlightenment by meditating, without bothering about emotional catharsis.

First you should consider that the psychological environment of Hindu disciples half a century ago cannot be compared to that of a seeker brought up today in Los Angeles or Milan. Our civilisation has reached an unprecedented level of neurosis, and **before trying to become supernormal, it is wise to work at becoming normal**. As long as the Daddy-Mummy, girlfriend-boyfriend level of existence has not been sorted out, why fool oneself by pretending to live a divine life? Such an attitude would mean running the risk of meditating for fifty years without any real breakthrough, simply because the tangled webs of your reacting mind can in no way be compared to the emotional simplicity of Indian people a few decades ago. Nowadays India has changed a lot, and the level of neurosis of its people is not very different from ours.

Apart from that, it would be utterly untrue to say that Hindu or Buddhist disciples did not have to go through a long and painful process of emotional catharsis before stepping into their glorious meditation. But this work on samskaras was done in a different way.

Finding a teacher was not an easy enterprise. In India or Tibet until not so long ago, would-be disciples often had to travel for several years and face all kinds of perils before they could reach a teacher – which represented an initiatory trial in itself.

117

Having found the guru, the disciples' troubles had only just begun. The Hindu and Buddhist traditions are full of stories of masters who drove their disciples to the borderline of insanity in order to help them get rid of their mental preconceptions and their samskaras. Only after having been 'cooked' like this for years would the disciple be given initiation.

Take the story of the great master Milarepa, for instance. During his years of preparation his guru, Marpa, asked him to build a circular house on a hill, after which Milarepa was to receive initiation. When Milarepa had built half the house, Marpa came back and said, "Look son, I think this is not really a good place for a house. So demolish it and put the stones back where you got them." Milarepa found the news difficult to cope with, but did as he was told. A week later, Marpa took Milarepa onto another hill and told him, "This is where I want the house, and it should be semi-circular." Anxious to receive his initiation, Milarepa started the new building immediately.

When Milarepa had erected about half of the semi-circular house, Marpa came back and said, "What is this ridiculous shack you are building here?" Milarepa was bewildered, and when he managed to articulate that he was only following the instructions he had been given, Marpa answered, "Did I say that? I must have been drunk that day. But today I am not drunk, and I have had a good think about the house. A Tantric mystical building should be triangular. So you will demolish your shack, carry all the stones to this other hill, and build me a triangular tantric house." Milarepa nearly collapsed when he heard these words. Marpa, drunk, how could that be! And the house to be rebuilt again! Milarepa was exhausted, his hands were full of blisters, and he had a big wound on his back, which he did not want to show Marpa for fear of displeasing him. Milarepa was disheartened and confused, but he really wanted to find Truth. He had two choices, either leave and renounce initiation, or trust Marpa unconditionally and keep on building. So he gathered his last forces, and started demolishing his beautiful semi-circular house, carrying the stones to the other hill.

After Milarepa had completed about a third of the triangular house, Marpa arrived on the site. He looked very angry. He shouted, "You filthy sorcerer! Do you realise that the shape of this building is going to attract all the demons of the area? Are you trying to destroy me and my family? Who told you to build such a monstrous house?" Overcome with despair, Milarepa could hardly answer, "But you asked me to!" Marpa was getting angrier and angrier. "Ignominious liar!" he said, "I never ordered that! How can you be so insolent? And you would like me to initiate you! Demolish this house immediately and put the stones back where you found them!" Then Marpa left. The night that followed was a moonless night – the darkest night of Milarepa's entire life. He was purely and simply cracking up; his whole mental structure was being shattered. But for some reason he did not leave.

The following morning, Marpa sent his wife to get Milarepa. They fed him a good meal, and suddenly Milarepa saw his troubles coming to an end, thinking he was going to be initiated. Not at all! Marpa kept him building and demolishing houses for years, some square, some nine storeys high, and he used many other subterfuges to throw Milarepa into constant pangs of desperation. Milarepa nearly committed suicide a number of times.

Then one day the path of disintegration was completed, and to his greatest surprise, Milarepa suddenly received the long-awaited initiation. After this Milarepa became one of the most enlightened gurus of the Tibetan tradition.

Similar stories, in which gurus put their disciples in impossible situations in order to help them work out their samskaras, could fill entire books. These trials can be regarded as an equivalent of the work done through regression – which, seen from this new perspective, is not so hard after all!

10.3 How come so many people seem to find out that they have been somebody important in a past life?

Precisely, they don't! After having witnessed thousands of regressions with clients and students of the Clairvision School, I have only come across *one* person who reexperienced having been a member of a royal family in Europe. The statement that everyone discovers they were someone important in a past life is a fanciful one, usually supported by people who do not have the faintest experience of true regression.

10.4 How come, when reexperiencing a past life, people do not start speaking in the language that was theirs in that life?

Before coming to Australia, I lived in France for twenty-seven years. French was my mother tongue. Then I came to adopt English as a language that felt more natural to me.

I have had an experience several times, which may shed some light on this question. When remembering episodes or conversations that took place in France – and in French – it often happens that the words come back to me in English! If this transfer of language may happen within one life, it is quite easy to conceive that it may also happen from one incarnation to another.

Perhaps we do not realise exactly what language is about. We think languages are made of words. But maybe languages are made of forces, and the words we put on top of these forces to express them are of less importance than the forces themselves. When we die the words fall, but the forces remain, and we carry them with us from life to life. People who are used to operating in more than one language at a time will probably find it easy to relate to this concept.

CONCLUSION

To conclude this study of the mechanisms of regression, I will extend both an invitation and a warning.

First, the invitation. What if your life could be completely transformed by a regression process? Could it be that what we have discussed in this book also applies to you? Could it be that, unknown to you, your life is presently influenced by some major samskaras, and that by revealing these samskaras and working them out, completely new avenues would open in your life?

Next, the warning. If you are to undergo a regression process, make sure you do it with a qualified connector. In particular, the direction of the process should be to reach clarity in your present life, rather than write novels about your past lives. Having understood the sound principles presented in this book, you will be able to detect the less serious practitioners (those who are only too happy to tell you that you have been a king or a queen in your past lives) and stay away from them.

If you wish to know more about ISIS, you can obtain publications and other learning material from the Clairvision School's Internet site. (The address is indicated at the end of the introduction.)

I wish you the best in your quest.

INDEX

Index